PONTIAC FIREBIRD

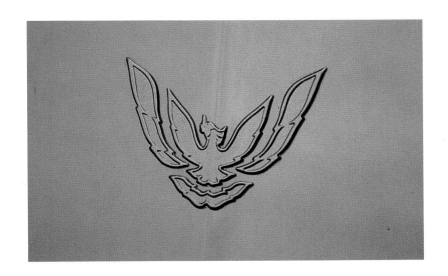

PONTIAC FIREBIRD

Nicky Wright

OSPREY
AUTOMOTIVE

First published in Great Britain in 1995
by Osprey, an imprint of Reed Consumer
Books Limited, Michelin House,
81 Fulham Road, London SW3 6RB and
Auckland, Melbourne, Singapore and Toronto.

ISBN 1 85532 340 0

Project editor Shaun Barrington
Editor Julia North
Page design Paul Kime/Ward Peacock
Partnership

Produced by Mandarin Offset
Printed in Hong Kong

ACKNOWLEDGEMENTS

There follows a list of car owners and all the people who helped in putting this book together. To all of them my eternal thanks.
Rick Choler, Dick Choler, Greg Choler, Bill Goodsene, Dorothy Gilbert, Keith Wilson, Joe & Mary Pieragustini, Pete Fultz, Robert H. Bennett, Mike Kollver, Jon Chevalier, Matt Leon, William J. Heerschop, John Hamlin, Christine Jo Bennett, Randy & Tina Gobbel, Gregg Anderer, Matt & Molly Leon, Jan Mueller, Beth Anderer, Stewart Meredith, Dale E. Varner, Dick Collier, Pontiac Motor Division, Shayla Smith, Randy Fox, Rick Asher, all of Pontiac PR, Marshall Police Department, Marshall, Michigan, National Motor Museum, Beaulieu, Hants, U.K., Larry Keiser, Brooks Field Airport, Marshall, Michigan, Jan Mueller, Police chief Roger Graves, Marshall, MI., Mary Jenkins, and all those wonderful British Trans Am owners who let me photograph their cars at the 1992 pre-'50 AAC R.O.G.

My thanks also, to William Porter, Buick chief of design, and Wayne Vieira, Saturn chief of design, for their reminiscences and patience. And I mustn't forget John Schinella, who, like Bill Porter and Wayne Vieira, was a major influence on Firebird design ... my grateful thanks.

Very special thanks to my wife, Becky, for her untiring help and patience.

All photographs taken on Fuji film, and shot with Pentax 6 x 7 and 645 cameras. All detail work and special effects shot with Nikon cameras.

This book is respectfully dedicated to the Trans Am Club of America, Michigan chapter ... not forgetting, of course, all those wonderful Firebirds, Formulas, and Trans Ams grunting their merry way along the roads of the world. Brrrm, brrm.

For a catalogue of all books published by Osprey Automotive
please write to:

The Marketing Department, Reed Consumer Books,
1st Floor, Michelin House, 81 Fulham Road, London SW3 6RB

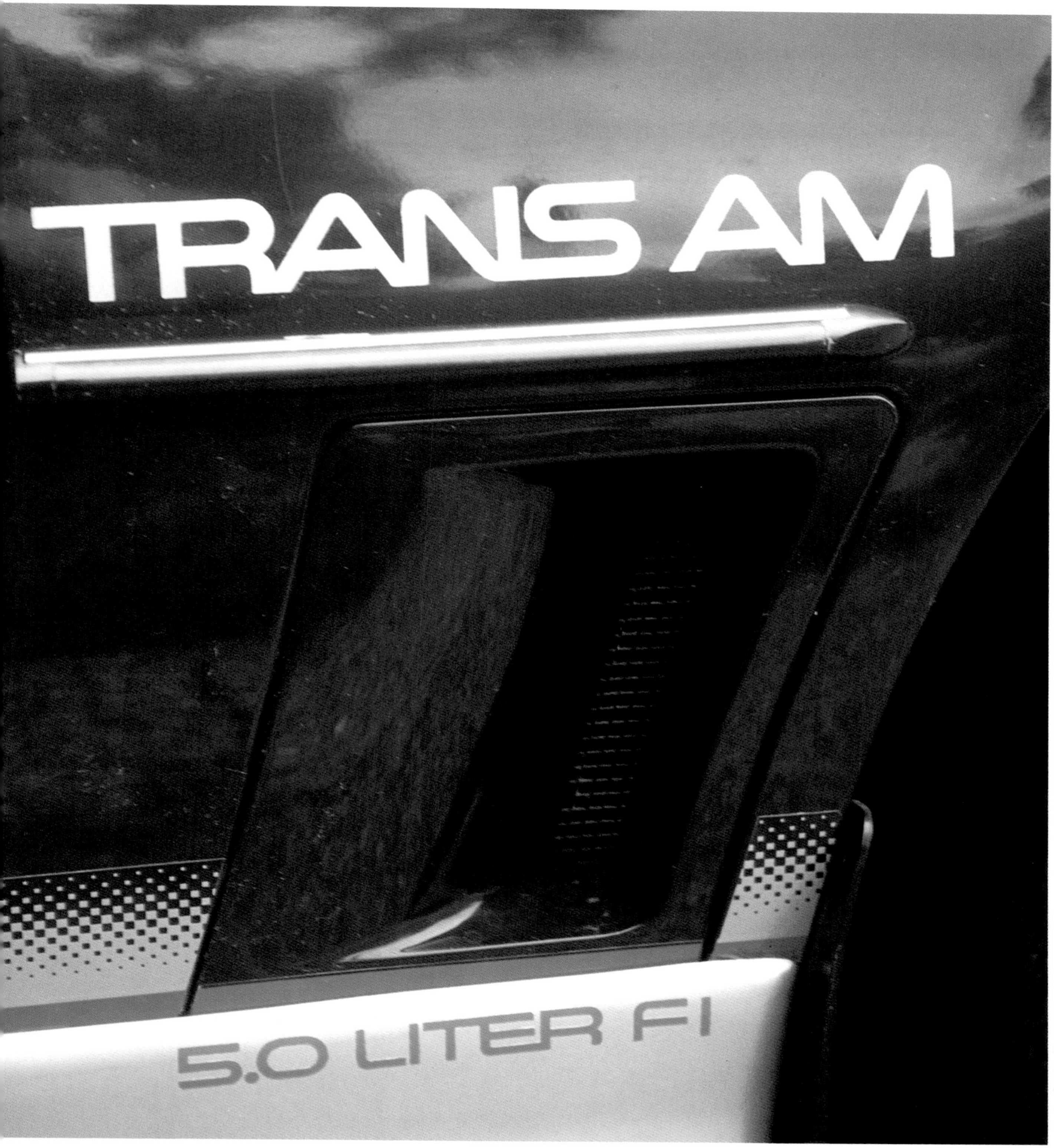
TRANS AM
5.0 LITER FI

Contents

Half-title page
From its very beginnings in 1926, Pontiac has always espoused native American culture. Big Chief Pontiac posthumously gave his name, though it's unlikely anyone thought of asking what might have remained of his family. Today the Chief no longer proudly crests a Pontiac grille but the Indian tradition continues in the form of stylized 'firebirds' on the noses of Firebirds and Trans Ams. This one is an early nineties variation

Title page
The car with an 'attitude'. Or how Pontiac liked to describe the 1992 Trans Am in its final year with the third generation body. A generous 1991 facelift gave the car a softer, more sensual front-end appearance

Right
All new split grilles and changed outer skins distinguished the 1969/70 Firebirds from its 1967/68 predecessors. Welcome improvements were single-piston power front disc brakes costing $64.95 extra if the buyer ordered them. 11,649 convertibles were produced in 1969/70

Fourth Out of the Trap

On April 17th 1964, Ford dropped a bombshell on the doorsteps of every automobile manufacturer in the U.S.A. With much hullabaloo they introduced the very sporty, youthful Mustang. With Ford General Manager, Lee Iacocca, beaming in the wings, the Mustang proceeded to break all new car sales records – it sold a massive 760,000 units in its first eighteen months. Handsome, and as spirited as the pony who inspired its name, the Mustang galloped into every red blooded American youngster's heart ... and quite a few older ones too.

Available at the rock bottom price of $2,368 in standard six-cylinder form, the Mustang changed American automotive thinking overnight. Apart from the Corvette, sportscars were not built in America. The original two-seater Thunderbird was termed a 'personal car' by Ford, who turned a beautiful design into a four-seater baroque-mobile for the nouveau riche. If Americans wanted a sports type car – and there were many who did – they had to turn to Europe.

The Mustang changed all that. Though not considered a true sportscar in the accepted sense, it was a reasonable size and fun to drive. If the buyer specified a V-8 and optional handling suspension, the Mustang handled quite well, and certainly better than the huge cars that used to wallow all over the interstates like hippos in a mud pool.

It is pretty obvious that when GM, Chrysler and American Motors saw Ford's fleet little car in the showrooms, press, and increasingly on the roads, they were mortified. Chevrolet, whose battles to the death with Ford were legendary, wasn't too worried at the outset. After all, America's No.1 had a restyled, much improved Corvair coming out for 1965, and initially thought it would be enough to stem the tide. At least Chevrolet could comfort themselves with the thought that the Mustang was in part a reaction to the Corvair – especially the attractive and very sporty Monza.

Between April and August 1965, Mustangs were pouring onto the road at the rate of almost a thousand a day. GM realized by now that the new Corvair was too different, too radical, couldn't be had with V-8

The car that started it all, the 1964 Mustang, seen here in convertible form. Caught napping, GM rushed Chevrolet and Pontiac to the drawing boards to create what became known as the Camaro and Firebird. By the time they hit the showrooms in 1967, Ford had already sold over a million Mustangs

power and was costlier to build. Meetings took place between GM's top brass and Chevrolet officials in an effort to resolve what could be done. Accord was reached: in the autumn of 1964 Chevrolet embarked upon the F-Car, also coded as Project Panther, a programme to produce an answer to the phenomenally successful Mustang.

Meanwhile, over at Pontiac, general manager John Z. (for Zachery) DeLorean and his engineering colleagues had been working on XP-833, a two-seater sportscar that would have an all fibreglass body. Work had begun on this idea in August 1963, a concept that was very dear to DeLorean's heart. But, try as he may, he could not convince the powers-that-be that XP-833 would do wonders for Pontiac; they felt it might offend Chevrolet who already had the Corvette. There was no room for a similar vehicle.

DeLorean wasn't too keen to become involved with a four-seater, Mustang-type sporty car such as Chevrolet was developing, and continued to push for his two-seater. After a few months he realized he was beating his head against the proverbial brick wall, and reluctantly began to look at the F-Car. Corporate heads thought a Pontiac version of the F-Car would help allay the initial development costs, so invited DeLorean to rejoin the program. (Pontiac had been involved with the F-Car in a minor way at the outset.)

By the time Pontiac decided to go for its own pony car, Chevrolet had all but completed theirs. The Camaro was to be in Chevrolet show rooms by 20 October 1966, but the Banshee, (of which more later) as everyone thought the new car would be called, was slated for early 1967.

Work began on Pontiac's version of the F-Car during March 1966. This didn't allow Pontiac stylists, headed by Jack Humbert, much time to give the Camaro body a separate identity. Fortunately for Pontiac, what are known as long-lead-time sheet metal releases such as structural pieces, cowl, floorpan, inner doors, etc., had already been formed by Chevrolet. Therefore, Pontiac's engineers and designers only had to worry about short-lead-time parts that didn't take long to develop. Items such as hood, trunk end panel, and grille would fit this catagory.

Chevrolet engineers, who were aware that Ford had borrowed from the compact Falcon to build the Mustang, looked at the Chevy II as a possible donor for the Camaro. The Chevy II was a unitized body/frame structure with a bolt-on front end. The independent front suspension had double-acting shock absorbers mounted inside the front coil springs and the coils were affixed to the upper A-arms. This, the engineers decided, was not how the Camaro would be, as the Chevy II's layout resulted in what might be termed a crude ride – in other words, rough and noisy.

A completely new design was worked out by using a front sub-frame

to carry engine, transmission, and the suspension parts, the coils attached to the lower control arms, and isolating the frame with rubber bushings. The main body section, from the cowl back, was unitized. At the rear, the engineers employed a Salisbury solid axle, tubular shocks, and Chevy II's single leaf springs. The result was a better ride, approaching certain sporty-type vehicles coming out of Europe.

Engines ranged from Chevrolet's 230 cubic inch OHV straight six to a 350 cid V-8. Wheelbase was 108 in. (9 ft.) and overall length was 184.6 in. (15 ft. 3 in.). Two bodystyles were available: a coupé and convertible, the base coupé with a three-speed manual box coupled to the 140 hp six retailed at $2,466. And following Mustang's lead, the Camaro could be loaded to the gills from an options list as tall as the Empire State!

Having decided to go with the F-body so late in development, Pontiac

Above
Front buckets came as standard on 1967 Firebirds, but $31.60 would buy a bench seat called the Strato-Bench. This option added extra passenger space which no doubt didn't go unnoticed by youngsters out on a Friday night date

Left
The dictates of fashion called for vinyl roofs, despite the reluctance of designers to implement them, especially on sporty cars like the 1967 Firebird. Black, ivory or cream were the choice of colours for this $84.26 option

found it didn't have much time to turn the car into a distinctive entity. The stylists played around with several front-end ideas based upon Pontiac's traditional (since 1959) split grille, before settling on chrome framed 'nostrils' flanked by dual headlights. A central 'pinched nose' effect added a further four inches over the Camaro's length.

"We had some excruciating problems with the front bumper/grille arrangement." Wayne Vieira, now chief stylist with Saturn cars, was a young designer working under Pontiac studio chief, Jack Humbert, and was involved with the design of the first and second generation Firebirds, the name finally settled upon for Pontiac's F-car.

"The lower valence," observed Vieira, studying a photograph of the first Firebird, "and the front fender are Chevrolet Camaro parts. Yet if you look at the Camaro parts you would say, well it's completely different. There's a big opening here. The headlamps are different, the location is different.

"Yes, they do look different, but we had a lot of hard work executing this chrome bumper which was unique (the bumper was the chromed frame around the split grille). Incidentally, the idea for this arrangement came from a sketch done by designer Dave Clark – and I executed it into clay. Clark was a very gifted designer who had an affinity for doing beautiful line work which Bill Mitchell approved of." (Bill Mitchell was the brilliant, but somewhat overpowering vice-president of GM design.)

"Clark had a nice swing to his hand," continued Vieira, "and essentially did that design. We had to put a little chrome flap to cover up the lower part of the Chevrolet design which we wouldn't normally do, but it was all part of what we had to do to make the bumper/grille design work. Another thing, the grilles are plastic; Pontiac was deeply into plastic grilles by this time and the rest of the industry hadn't caught up with us yet."

A nice touch was the hood treatment on the Firebird. William (Bill) Porter, now Buick's chief designer and the man responsible for the 1995 Riviera, took over Pontiac styling when Jack Humbert left and refers to the treatment as the 'ironing board' affect. "Wayne Vieira was responsible for the Firebird's hood, the slightly raised center section flowing from the cowl forward to continue into the bumper's beak.

"I did the 'ironing board', said Vieira. "This had to do with sharing the windshield wiper location and cowl vents. Herb Kaiser, a Pontiac executive engineer, came in one day just as I was about to leave. He said

Another view of the '67 with the Cordova top. Much of the earlier Firebird's body was shared with Chevrolet's Camaro, yet Pontiac designers managed to achieve a distinctive look for their car. Wheels are incorrect and come from a later Firebird

'we can't figure out how to get this windshield wiper in there'.

"My reply was to put a slot at the wiper locating points, so Herb and I sat down and we designed the whole thing in two or three minutes. That's how the 'ironing board' came about."

Once Wayne Vieira and Pontiac's design staff had finished with the design, the Firebird looked a different car from the Camaro, both at front and rear. Narrow twin horizontal taillights on either side, set in a distinctive rear panel, were more graceful than Camaro's larger, one-piece units. Six vertical scoops riding three abreast on the upper and lower portions of the rear fenders, helped separate the Firebird from the Camaro on the body sides.

Before looking at the range of models and engines proposed for Pontiac's pony car, a name that came about with the birth of the Mustang for obvious reasons, let's consider the name, 'Firebird'.

Above
One way to distinguish the little-changed 1968 Firebird from the '67, was the absence of windwings as clearly seen above. Pontiac coyly called the absence 'Astro-Ventilation'. This view is how most people first saw a Firebird

Right
This view illustrates the handsome bumper-grille combination of the first generation Firebird. Note controversial 'ironing board' styling cue on the hood; Bill Mitchell thought this an important part of the Firebird's identity to further separate it from Camaro

At the time, everybody thought the car would be christened 'Banshee', after the four-seater styling exercise following Pontiac's two place roadsters that DeLorean was so keen on. In fact, DeLorean had already made up his mind that Banshee was to be the name. It seemed appropriate for a sporty car to be christened after the Korean fighter plane officially known as the McDonnell Douglas F2H, and Pontiac even paid $6000 to a kit car company for the rights to the name. Then somebody looked up banshee in Webster's. It transpired that banshee was a "female spirit in Gaelic folklore whose wailing warns a family of an approaching death." Nobody, least of all the marketing people, wanted the car they were trying to sell to be known as a harbinger of death. What kind of image would that conjure up? And imagine the meal stand-up comedians would make out of a car with a name meaning death?

"'Banshee', recalled Vieira, "was a big name until somebody downtown looked it up and discovered it meant harbinger of death, and thought maybe it wasn't a good name for the car. You have to appreciate this was after the Nadar vision ... so-called ... (laughter). Can you imagine what would have happened when it got into the news? A name with a meaning like that! (more laughter.)

"I can remember the decision to make it Firebird," continued Vieira with prompting from Porter. "Everybody rebelled against the name because all they could remember were the turbine cars GM made, the Firebird models 1, 2, and 3. Nobody could associate it with the new car at first, but then the public probably had never heard of the Firebird turbine cars."

"I remember being very upset when I heard it was to be called the Firebird." explained Porter. "Very upset. I just thought it was a terrible idea: Oh, no! Why would they call it a Firebird? It's not a turbine car. It's a terrible idea!" (Laughter).

"Anyway, the name stuck," Porter said. Suddenly it was the Firebird; all the other cars were forgotten. You ask anyone today what a Firebird is and they know it is a Pontiac. You know, a name becomes what it is. The name becomes what the car is. In a very short time."

When the Firebird finally hit the showrooms on 23 February 1967, it arrived with the disadvantage of three other pony cars coming before it. First was the Mustang, then, almost two years later, Chevrolet's Camaro and the Mercury Cougar. Mustang had derived its success from a low base price and a barrelful of options to enable the buyer to build his Mustang the way he wanted it. Camaro followed the same theme, but the Cougar aimed for the luxury end of the sporty car spectrum, emphasizing a boulevard ride and all the creature comforts one would find in a Lincoln.

Pontiac's approach with the Firebird was entirely different. There

Above right
Another view of the '69 Trans Am (foreground) and Camaro SS. Standard engine for the '69-70 T/A was a 400 cid, 335 hp V8 that was very fast. Only 697 T/As were built during the extended 1969/70 season. The pane, by the way, is a German Fieseler Storch from WWII

Below right
On the left, a 1969 Trans Am. On the right, a 1969 Chevrolet Camaro SS. This was the first year for both the Trans Am and the SS, and apart from front and rear end differences, the cars' bodies are virtually the same

Above left
One-piece grille, enclosed headlights and almost flat hood. From '67–70, Camaro designers called the shots leaving Pontiac to make do with individual front and rear treatments for the F-Car body

Left
Side treatment differences were minor, restricted to placement of phony extractor-vents, ID emblems. Wheels were unique to the particular marque and interiors different. SS Camaro was the precursor to the later Z-28

Above
Power of the hour for Camaro's SS model was Chevrolet's potent 396 motor. Pontiac responded with the 400 cid, 335 hp V-8 thus pipping Chevy by a hair

were five models, each designed to suit whatever the buyer chose. The base car had a six-cylinder engine as standard equipment. Developing 165 bhp at 4700 rpm, the engine was unique to Detroit inasmuch as it was an overhead cam unit. Originally designed for the Tempest and GTO, the engine was technically quite advanced for an American car during the days when overhead valves were king.

Next came the Sprint. This again used the OHC six but rated at 215 bhp at 5200 rpm. This engine had a Quadrajet 4 bbl carburetor, different intake and exhaust manifolds, and a different cam. A three-speed manual shift came with both engines which had compression ratios of 9.0 and 10.5:1 respectively. In its latter guise, the OHC Sprint six gave a very good account of itself, with 0–60 arriving in about 10 seconds.

In the days when to shout 'gas economy' was tantamount to committing treason, big, heavy duty V8s ruled the American roost. So it goes without saying that the Firebird had its fair share of multicylinder blocks. The first was the 326 cid unit developing a respectable 250 hp in the Firebird 326 model. A single 2 bbl carburetor and 3-speed manual column shift didn't really make it with the go-faster brigade, who favoured the Firebird HO or Firebird 400.

Both autos could display plenty of muscle when the traffic-lights turned to green, the 325 horse Firebird 400 being the quickest. The

HO's engine wasn't quite so powerful with 285 horses, but it had dual exhausts, and the same 4 bbl carburetor. Actually, the horsepower was probably quite a bit more than the advertised figure, but due to an odd GM ruling current during the '60s, no production engine was allowed to produce more than 1 hp for every 10 lbs of vehicle weight.

It goes without saying that Pontiac engineers modified the suspension to suit whatever engine was under the hood. Although the base suspension was very similar to the Camaro's, Firebirds were superior in handling and ride due to the changes made.

One difference was the use of traction bars at the rear. As has already been mentioned, the F-body was stuck with Chevy II's single leaf springs essentially because of the cost considerations. This really was a false economy because so much else had to be done to prevent wheel hop, axle judder, and wheelspin – unpleasant habits endemic to this type of

Above
Five spoke, five lug Rally II wheels were standard on the 1969 Trans Am, an option on other Firebirds. Radial tires were still to come on American cars as factory equipment; Goodyear Polyglas bias-belted rubbers were Pontiac's best option in '69

Left
Note how the 'ironing board' disappears when functional hood scoops are added. Scoops, fake side extractors and rear spoiler were originally by California customiser Gene Winfield, and designer Harry Bradley. Piper aircraft in background

suspension. Especially when a lot of power is being applied to the rear.

Considering what they had to work with, Pontiac's engineering team did a remarkable job in turning a relatively crude system into one that could perform. Initially, they added a pair of traction bars (as opposed to only one on the Camaro). Next to each bar is a bracket attached to the Hotchkiss solid axle housing and extending along their lengths. Each bar is cushioned by a length of rubber in between, and each arm makes contact with its companion near the middle. The purpose of all this was to prevent axle rotation, or wind up under hard acceleration or braking. An interesting point: the Firebird's bars were adjustable by turning a small bolt, resulting in the degree of loading being altered to suit the driver's whim.

Twin traction bars were not available on all Firebird models; only the 400 manual and automatic, 326 manual, and 4 bbl ohc six. A single bar was used on the 326 and ohc six with automatic transmissions, and none at all on the plain-jane single barrel ohc six. Isolated from metal surfaces by a series of rubber bushings, the Firebird's suspension was surprisingly supple with none of the harshness normally associated with stiffened leaf sprung systems.

Affectionately known as 'The Magnificent Five' (obviously thought up by a fan of the western movie *The Magnificent Seven!*), the Firebirds met with an enthusiastic response from the public. Of the 82,558 Firebirds sold in what was a rather short model year, most were equipped with the smaller V-8. Only 17,664 six-cylinder cars were produced. Compared to the larger displacement V-8s, while the ohc six didn't have the acceleration or speed, it weighed less, thus offsetting its power limitations with a combination of better weight distribution, handling and ride. Unfortunately, in those days, only automotive experts appreciated anything remotely sophisticated; as far as Joe Public was concerned there was no substitute for cubic inches, hence the popularity of the ohv V-8.

Not that there was anything wrong with torquey V-8 power. *Motor Trend* magazine tested a 325 horse, 400 cid V-8 powered Firebird in their March 1967 issue. Torque was a massive 410 at 3400 rpm, and the testers managed a respectable 0–60 time of 7.5 seconds out of the car. It took 15.4 seconds and 92 mph to run the quarter mile. Not bad for a car weighing in excess of 3850 lbs.

The magazine also tried out the Sprint with the 215 hp ohc six under the hood. This had a four-speed manual (the 400 came with a three-speed Turbo-Hydramatic) and moved gracefully to 60 in 11.1 seconds. Not bad, but not good either, especially when compared to modern six-cylinder engines. In the sixties, though, six-cylinder engines took a back seat when it came to performance.

Nobody liked the inclusion of GM's two-speed automatic as an option

Above right
First year production found all Trans Ams painted white with dark blue stripes, the latter added somewhat reluctantly by designer Bill Porter. Porter's team wanted function, not pizzazz, but had to compromise. Special Projects engineer Herb Adams, and assistant chief engineer Bill Collins elected to have more garish striping

Below right
Standard Ram-Air 400 V-8 leaves little room under hood of 1969 Trans Am. A driver-controlled underdash knob regulated cold/warm air mixture to engine through hood scoops. 345 hp L-67 Ram-Air IV was rare option: only 46 T/As had this engine in 1969

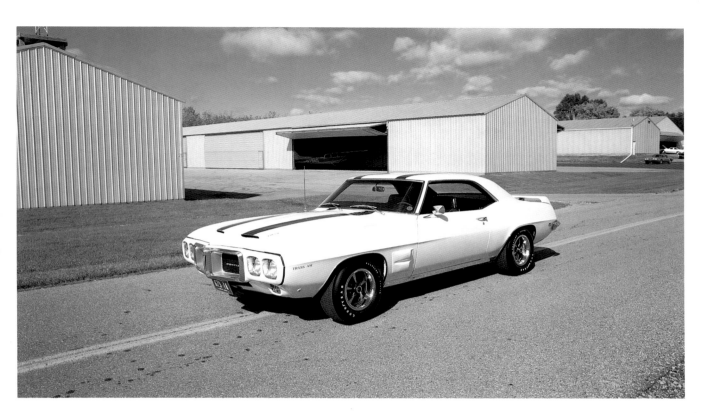

for the six and 326 V-8 models. Why it was offered is anybody's guess. Probably Pontiac wanted to make sure all its bases were covered. As it turned out there were many who bought the Firebird because they liked the look and style of a car that was equally at home on a boulevard as it was 'getting the lead out'.

For blood and guts, motoring buyers could order the optional Ram-Air package – available only on the 400. Functional twin hood scoops sucked in dollops of air to assist in cooling this very hot motor down. With the Ram-Air package the buyer got a hotter cam, longer valve duration, valve springs with metal dampers, and a free flowing cast iron exhaust. A deep breathing Quadra-Jet four barrel carburetor rounded out this exciting engine. Motoring journalists found that the Ram-Air package sliced almost a full second off the 0–60 times posted by the Firebird 400 without Ram-Air.

Above
This is the base L-30 350 V-8 developing 265 hp found in many '69/70 Firebirds. There were eight different engine variations to choose from, beginning with the 250 cid ohc six (in its final year), and ending with the 400 cube 345 hp Ram-Air IV

Right
11,649 Firebird convertibles were made during the 1969/1970 model year, the 1969 car shown being one of them. Low angle view enhances the well-proportioned lines of the car. Fake wire wheel covers optional; emissions equipment became standard

Unlike Europe, where cars had made use of disc brakes for 15 years, they were still in their infancy in the America of the mid-sixties. Safety, it seemed, had no argument against cost; Crosley and Chrysler had both tried disc brakes in 1947 and 1951 respectively, yet cast them aside. Thunderbird and Corvette offered discs on all four wheels from 1964, much to their credit. But the standard brakes on a 1967 Firebird were drums with front discs as an option.

An interesting and unusual touch was the hood-mounted tachometer. After having designed the interior, the stylists found there wasn't enough room for the tach. Putting it on the hood was Wayne Vieira's, and the then assistant chief designer, Ron Hill's idea. "We wanted a tach," said Vieira. "We couldn't put it on the inside of the car so we decided to put it on the outside. So I did the sketches and we executed the design ... Bill Mitchell thought the design was great; it was a neat thing for the car", continued Vieira. "In actual fact it was terrible. You couldn't read the thing through the windshield if it was raining or if it was dirty, and at nighttime it was useless. But kids loved it ... and still do."

Of course the tach didn't come as standard; it cost $63.19 if the buyer wanted it. In fact, to make any car worthwhile in the sixties, one would have to study the options book. Very little came as standard in those days, and the Firebird was no exception. A base Firebird cost what looked like a bargain $2,666. For that, the buyer got the 165 hp ohc six, three speed column shift, bucket seats, heater, E70-14 Wide Oval tires, a space-saver spare, and carpeting. For only a little more ($3,109), the buyer could have heavy duty suspension, heavy duty floor mounted three speed manual, dual exhausts, and the 400 V-8 engine. After that, the sky was the limit. For a little over $4,000, one could have the Ram-Air package which consisted of twin functioning hood scoops – on the 400 the scoops were for decoration only – engine modifications already discussed elsewhere, and limited slip differential, Rally I or Rally II wheels, power front disc brakes, power steering, four-speed manual or Turbo-Hydramatic, and the hood mounted tach. Power windows, Custom-Aire conditioning, and floor mounted centre console unit would add a further $456,03. Which really wasn't too bad for a car capable of 0–60 in under seven seconds.

Considering the opposing camps' pony car offerings, the Firebird did very well in its first, albeit shortened, model year. 82,560 units were sold, which wasn't far off John DeLorean's predicted 100,000 figure. It may be of interest to know that a mere 63 Ram Air coupes and two convertibles were built that first year. Anybody who has one is sitting on a very nice investment indeed! As for the rest of them, all had the advantage of a full model year's production. The Camaro managed 220,906 against Mustang's 472,121. As for the Cougar, it chalked up 150,983 sales, thus

Above right
Aggressive grille which highlighted 1969 facelift, brings to mind a pinched nose with flaring nostrils. Heavy chrome look disappeared after one season. Ponycar sales were down in '69, so Pontiac reduced Firebird prices by $72 to encourage buyers

Below right
Energy-absorbing steering column and seat head rests were part of the safety requirements initiated by a government decree in 1968. Head rests can be seen in '69 Firebird shown here. Orange hue was one of 15 standard colors offered in 1969

giving Ford an unbeatable two to one margin over GM and Chrysler combined. As for Chrysler, well, Plymouth had its Barracuda, an attractive little car nobody took much notice of. Still, it sold 62,534 units.

Vent windows disappeared, side marker lamps designed like the Pontiac logo appeared on the rear fenders (they were almost square at the front), and a few interior changes marked the differences between the 1967 and 1968 Firebird models. Most changes took place under the hood and in the rear suspension. The 326 engine was replaced by a new 350 V-8 which had redesigned heads and larger, more upright valves which were spaced further apart. Developed horsepower at 5100 rpm was 320.

Two additional 400 cid engines were offered. Bore and stroke was identical on all four, at 4.12 x 3.75, and torque was almost the same. The most powerful 400 was the L-67 Ram Air II which developed 340 bhp at 5300 rpm. Both the L-67 Ram Air and L-74 400 HO developed 335 leaving the W-66 Base 400 at 330 horses. The base ohc six jumped to 175 hp and added 20 more cubic inches.

One of the problems owners encountered with the '67 Firebirds was rear axle wheel hop under hard acceleration, especially with one of the big V-8s under the hood. As we have already seen, Pontiac engineers tried everything they could to minimize the problem without over-extending the corporate budget. Rubber bushed, adjustable traction bars helped but didn't cure. If one was to believe contemporary auto magazine reports, Pontiac alleviated the problem entirely: " … previous experience with single leaf springs caused us to expect trouble with wheel hop or at least wheelspin, neither of which ever materialized" enthused one road test.

Whatever the magazines might have said didn't cut much ice with Pontiac's engineers who insisted there was a malady that required immediate surgery. For 1968, the surgery consisted of non-symmetrical multi-leaf rear springs using four and five leaves. The shocks were biased with the one on the left mounted behind the axle, the right one in front of it. Traction bars were redundant now the Firebird had a superior rear suspension that cured wheel hop if not wheel spin, the latter being the nature of the beast with live axles and heavy engines.

1963 was the beginning of a social revolution that spanned the world. The start of a decade of change orchestrated by the Beatles, Rolling Stones, and Jimi Hendrix who, without realizing it, became the spiritual leaders of a youth movement protesting against 'the establishment'. There was also a small country tucked away in Southeast Asia called Vietnam. Small, maybe, but by 1968 it had torn America apart at the seams. Then there was the Timothy Leary drug culture: 'tune in, turn on, and drop out' was Leary's rallying cry as thousands of America's young

Above right
Twin sectioned taillights had back-up lights mounted in the centre, and were a very neat piece of styling resulting in a clean, uncomplicated rear. Considering the paranoia surrounding safety, it is odd nobody mandated amber turn signals

Below right
Another '69 convertible, this one sporting the popular Rally II wheels. Pontiac advertised the Firebird as "A sports car that rides as good as it looks", though some road testers didn't entirely agree. As a highway cruiser the Firebird scored top marks

did just that. San Francisco's Haight Ashbury became the 'flower power' kingdom, the LSD capital of the world. In 1968 alone, there was the Mai-Lai massacre, the assassinations of Martin Luther King and Bobby Kennedy and the brutal crushing of Czechoslovakia by Soviet forces.

One could argue that the automobile industry was also affected by the events round the world. The entire pony/muscle car boom owed its existence to the young; even the advertisements were couched in copy aimed at the youth market. Though a little more conservative than some, the Firebird kept in step with the times. One 1967 advertisement featured a coupé at the top of the page, a convertible at the bottom. The prose began under the coupé, thus: "Anything our light heavyweight can't handle … ", then above the convertible: "our heavyweight can." This was followed by copy obviously meant to thrill the college graduate: "Firebird HO. The HO on that sleek machine above means High Output. And

Above
Two Firebird diecast emblems were used in 1969, one for the rear sidemarker lights, the other as the trunk lock (above). Firebird emblem has Indian heritage but the inspiration came from a mural decorating a wall at Phoenix Skyway airport

Right
The Firebird's clean lines are shown off to advantage in this rear view shot of 1969 convertible. Minor modifications such as rear spoiler, elongated dual exhausts denote this car is not entirely stock...only the Trans Am had a spoiler in '69

what it means is a 326 cu. in. 285 hp V-8 with dual exhausts that blow the sweetest music this side of Sebring ... " And so on. In 1968 the advertising copy continued in much the same youthful vein to good effect. Production of the '68s rose to 107,112 in spite of another pretender to the ponycar throne from a most unlikely source. American Motors had dispensed with its maiden aunt image and came roaring out of its corner with the sleek, powerful Javelin.

Richard Milhous Nixon ended the troubled year of 1968 by narrowly winning the election for President of the United States. That he won was probably due in part to those who wanted to keep the status quo, which meant bringing the rebellious youth to heel. Somehow this attitude didn't quite make it into Detroit where the car manufacturers were just beginning to unleash some of the most fearsome muscle cars onto the 1969 marketplace.

1969 was probably the peak for out-and-out street power on wheels, almost a last 'hurrah' for an industry which had been ordered to clean up its act. Ralph Nader had won his battle; the carmakers had to comply with stringent safety and emissions controls passed by Congress in order to make the cars safer. The new measures, which started with side marker lights and California emissions equipment in 1968, continued in 1969 with headrests as standard by mid-year, a redesigned – in Pontiac's case – collapsible steering column, and the ignition key moved from the dashboard to the side of the steering column.

An entirely new grille, that reminded one of somebody pursing his lips under his nose, identified the new styling of the '69 Firebird. A thick chrome frame split by a beak in the middle was not, according to Wayne Vieira, the way it was originally designed: "This, as Bill (Porter) says, is not a particularly good front end," said Vieira looking over a photograph of a 1969 Firebird. "We wanted chrome around the headlamps and a urethane front end. Originally this was all body colour ... ," Vieira stabs his finger at the picture, " ... and the chrome was on the outside round the lamps. When Bill Mitchell saw the mock-up he shouted 'No! No! turn it around the other way. Put on a big chrome radiator shell'." Leaning back in his seat, Vieira chuckles at the memory of the incident.

"We weren't into the chrome thing," he continued. "Bill always felt strongly about chrome; he didn't like the Endura fronts because there was no chrome. He related to chrome radiator shells of the twenties and thirties and that is why the Firebird ended up with the chrome front and

Softer, rounded approach of 1970 Trans Am was initiated by Jack Humbert and carried through by Bill Portert. Distinctive body coloured bumper/grille adds a touch of class to a design that is intrinsically American, yet has European flair

Endura plastic surrounded the headlights." Pontiac's stylists were somewhat restricted with the facelift on the '69 Firebird because they had to adapt their designs to the lines already done by the Camaro designers. Flatter wheel arches, horizontal windsplits and a new roof line were the same as on the Camaro, but the Firebird at least had different front and rear ends. Three suspension systems were now offered on the Firebird – normal for six-cylinder cars, high rate for V-8s, and heavy duty for performance. The new suspensions were probably needed to cope with the increased horsepower given to all engines. The 250's ohc 6 base engine was now 215 hp, the optional one 230. There were two 350 cubic inch V-8s and three 400s, the largest developing 345 bhp.

No matter what sort of front end Bill Mitchell liked, the public didn't necessarily agree. Sales of the '69 Firebird dropped by almost 20,000 units over the previous year. To help sales gain some momentum Pontiac announced a price reduction averaging $72 for all Firebird models. But it wasn't something for nothing. By taking certain standard items such as the space saver spare, some trim embellishments, and the glovebox, and listing them as options, Pontiac made sure it wouldn't lose anything.

As we saw earlier, John DeLorean had originally wanted a two-seater sportscar cheaper than, but in competition with, the Corvette. Chevrolet screamed 'heresy' or words to that effect, and the idea entered the 'might have been' file. At least DeLorean had the hugely successful GTO and, latterly, the Firebird to promote Pontiac's sporty image. After the Firebird was launched in 1967, John DeLorean, advanced design engineer, William T. Collins, and Steve Malone, who was chief engineer, felt there was a need for an extra special Firebird, something racier and sportier than the normal line. Perhaps something to go racing with in the Trans Am series. To further this goal, Collins set up an advanced engineering wing within Pontiac's engineering section, and called it the Special Projects group. A gifted young engineer named Herb Adams was put in charge.

Auto racing was big business in the sixties – win on Sunday, sell on Monday, sort of thing. Everybody was doing it; if the car maker had a muscle or ponycar, it went racing, and Pontiac was no exception to this rule. However, it was the work of a dedicated Canadian millionaire, Terry Godsall, and sportscar magazine editor/racing driver, Jerry Titus, that convinced Pontiac to race Firebirds in the SCCA's Trans Am events. They formed the T/G Racing Team, running Canadian Firebirds – actually Camaros with a Firebird front end – in the Trans Am events. There was a valid reason why T/G raced Canadian Firebirds. SCCA rules wouldn't allow any engine over five litres, and Pontiac didn't have a V-8 that would qualify. As the Canadian Firebirds were really Camaros, they had Chevrolet's 302 cid V-8 which qualified.

Engine-turned aluminum panel highlights easily read white-on-black gauges. Clock set on the right of the 8000 rpm tachometer is a nice touch. Speedometer reads to 160 mph, a speed a shade optimistic even with the 400 Ram-Air III engine

Below right
Dual headlights were dropped in favour of single units for the 1970 Firebird/Trans Am cars, thus giving the front end a very clean, very visual look. Aerodynamic research proved T/A had superior handling when equipped with standard spoiler package

Using Z-28 302 engines in their hybrid Firebirds, Titus and Godsall continued to race while Pontiac wrestled with building a 5-litre of its own. A 303 cid V-8 resulted from destroking a 400 cid engine. Using Ram Air IV tunnelport heads – the Ram Air IV was the Firebird's most powerful engine – Adams and friends discovered an engine capable of producing 475 hp, fitting right in with the Trans Am competition. In 1969, after convincing the sceptical SCCA authority that they were putting the 303 into production – Pontiac had no intention of doing so because of the enormous expense to develop it for production cars – 25 models were built for racing. T/G put aside its hybrids to race the genuine Firebirds, though without much success, in 1970. Tragedy overtook T/G Racing when Jerry Titus was killed after an accident during practice for Road America, at Elkhart Lake, Wisconsin.

Even while Herb Adams and his Special Projects team were working on the 303, John DeLorean had approached Australian racing driver Jack Brabham and his Repco company, to build a 5-litre, overhead cam engine out of the 400 cid unit, suitable for SCCA. Five engines were contracted for and only one completed. Adams' work won the day, Pontiac paid off Brabham, and took delivery of the one 470 hp engine which now resides at General Motors Institute in Flint, Michigan.

All this development was leading, not just to competition, but DeLorean's real goal, which was the Trans Am. Herb Adams had learned a lot about performance through his work with T/G Racing, and was convinced a production Trans Am had to be. Finally, Adams, DeLorean, Malone, and others loyal to the concept, won out. Early in 1969, the Trans Am made its public debut at the Chicago Auto Show, eventually appearing in Pontiac showrooms a couple of months later, in early April. Although the Trans Am was Pontiac's answer to Mustang's Boss 302 and the Camaro Z-28, it received little fanfare upon its introduction. There wasn't even any sales literature to describe this as the very best of the Firebird range. Instead the new GTO Judge got all the publicity, possibly because Pontiac felt there was more potential with an intermediate at the time.

Whatever doubts Pontiac's hierachy may have felt about the Trans Am there was none from its creators. Their optimism would shortly pay off for it was soon recognized that the Trans Am represented the ultimate ponycar: stylish, with handling and performance far superior to the ordinary Firebird. Standard under the hood was a Ram-Air, 335 hp, 400 cubic inch V-8, although an extra 10 hp could be had by specifying the Ram-Air IV V-8. Suspension was heavy duty, the standard transmission a three-speed manual. A pair of four-speeds, one a close ratio box, and a Turbo-Hydra-Matic 400 automatic were options. GM's new variable ratio Saginaw power steering was precise and quick, needing only 2.5 turns

Trans Am got a rearward facing shaker hood scoop which really worked, a single blue stripe in place of the previous twins and a Firebird motif atop the grille. Decal was not that good on early examples, and didn't remain in place for very long. 3M later corrected the problem with a more durable decal

lock to lock. There was only one body colour – Camaro white with twin blue racing-style stripes that started at the twin, functional hood scoops and ended at the lip of the deck lid. A basket handle-type rear spoiler completed the picture.

Automotive editors were divided over the Trans Am. Some loved it, while others complained that the car was a Trans Am in name only. This was because it had a 400 engine rather than the promised – but never delivered – 303. Still, a couple of the magazines managed to crack the mile in a shade over 14 seconds at speeds of 100 mph, and while its handling may not have been up to competition racing, it was great for normal use. Even though the Trans Am sparked quite a bit of interest, it didn't help generate many extra sales in 1969. A late starter anyway, the Trans Am ended a very late model year with only 697 coupes and eight convertibles built. These are the rarest and probably the most sought after of the species today.

Due to engineering and tooling problems, introduction of the 1970 Firebirds was delayed until the end of February. Pontiac kept on selling 1969 Firebirds right up until the new model arrived, thus confusing some people into thinking a '69 was a 1970. Because the introduction of the new Firebird came so late, it was incorrectly labelled a 1970 model. Yet more confusion. Let's set the record straight: the car was a 1970 that was late in arriving. As we shall see, the wait was well worth it.

A Great American Sportscar

At about the time that the 1967 Firebird was being launched, work had already begun on the 1970, or second generation model. Whereas Pontiac designers had been restricted to making a few changes to an already complete Camaro design the first time, they had a much freer hand in giving the Firebird its own identity the second time around.

Much of the first generation Firebird's engineering was carried over into the new model although there was quite a bit of improvement on the mechanical side. Wheelbase remained unaltered, the V-8 engines were the same, albeit with different horsepower ratings. The 11 in. front disc brakes were taken off the option list and were made standard (a welcome move), and the 9.5 in. rear drums remained as before.

Nonetheless, engineering refinement was dramatic; while body width was narrowed a half inch, the Firebird's tread width was increased by 1.6 in. on models with V-8s, 0.3 in. on the six-cylinder cars. Spring rates were softened without sacrifice to ride or handling, partly due to the wider tread. There was considerable improvement to the steering linkage. First generation Firebirds had the linkage behind the axle centerline; the '70 models had the linkage placed ahead of the axle. Oversteer in hard turns had been present in earlier cars; now mild understeer was induced, thus making the Firebird easier for the everyday driver to control if the car got out of sorts.

Sadly Pontiac's excellent overhead-cam six was dropped. Sales hadn't been anything to rave about, and Pontiac considered the engine too expensive for relatively small volume production. Instead, Chevrolet's tried and true 250 cubic inch six became the Firebird's standard engine. As for the V-8s, they remained the same, though there were differences in horsepower ratings. The 350 cid V-8 was reduced to 255 hp while the more popular 400 now came in four sizes; 265, 330, 345, and 370 respectively. According to *Motor Trend*'s February 1970 road test of a 370 hp Trans Am, 0–60 was achieved in 6.5 seconds.

1972 Trans Am, little changed from 1970. Polycast honeycomb wheels were available from '71, but keen-eyed enthusiasts can spot a '72 by its grille which used honeycomb mesh. 1970-1971 had a square mesh design. Macho spoilers are much in evidence.

But the really big news was the Firebird's total body redesign. "It was one of the most beautiful cars we ever did" commented Bill Porter, Pontiac's chief designer who was largely responsible for the '70 Firebird. Porter replaced Jack Humbert in 1967, after Humbert had been promoted to executive designer in charge of both Pontiac and Chevrolet studios. Wayne Vieira, now chief designer for Saturn, was Humbert's assistant in those days and when Humbert moved on, became Bill Porter's assistant chief designer. Porter recalled his early days as a very young designer at Pontiac: "Humbert was a very good man to work for: we kind of cut our teeth with Jack. Bill Mitchell was the big boss, the tyrannical big boss. Jack was the studio chief and I worked for him from 1959 to 1961.

"I learned with Jack. He was an exquisite finisher. He had a remarkable eye for finishing; he was very fastidious." Wayne Vieira interjects: "That's the best part of Jack." Porter continues: "He was the most fastidious person around and I picked up a lot. In-so-far as my development as a designer went, I admire the fact that he could discern these tiny, tiny differences; the slightest flaw or imperfection Jack would spot instantly.

"He was a sort of an ideal for me for a number of years and as a result I had a great respect for him. I respected his abilities almost more than any other designer I worked with. He wasn't prone to the tantrums others got caught up with, and he'd pass along ideas he had to you if he wanted you to use them." Vieira: "I was very shy when I first came to the studio. I remember one occasion when I was sitting at the desk and I was doing a sketch showing louvres on the side of a car. I didn't realize that Jack was looking over my shoulder until he said 'Hey, that's pretty good. Why don't you do those louvres on the Le Mans for 1964? We'll make that the Le Mans identification'. And I did." Porter laughs: "So you're the guy who started the scoops thing." Vieira: "Yes, and I put them on the Firebird. Mitchell liked them and used to say, 'Let's put some good taste over there'."

What you have just read serves as an illustration as to why the 1970 Firebird was, and is, so highly regarded. Jack Humbert's influence on a pair of designers whose innate artistic abilities were already strong, was profound – as can be seen in the Firebird's design. Single headlights instead of duals, the radical endura front end, twin hood scoops (on some models), and a ride and handling package more akin to some European sportscars but at half the price, this was the second generation

A warm July day makes a perfect setting for this British-owned 1972 Trans Am. Here the results of freelance engineer Paul Lamar's aerodynamic research are apparent in the rounded lines of the car. Lamar worked with Pontiac as an independent contractor

Firebird. Pontiac's designers got a fair crack of the whip in the overall Firebird/Camaro concept, and were able to create in the Firebird a car that was considerably different from the Camaro. Doors, fenders, front and rear ends and hood, were unique to the Firebird. But it wasn't easy. Both Firebird and Camaro shared the same F-body platform, and each side had their ideas how the car should look. "The parts," recalled Vieira, "that didn't make it on the Firebird were the parts we had to compromise to make Chevrolet happy ..."

"Yes," said Porter. "The rear bumper had to be a little flatter; we wanted it more bladelike. We had a terrible scare from Bill Mitchell on one occasion. He came back from one of his trips and came in the studio and insisted on having a big 'ironing board' on the middle of the hood. He wanted an identity ..." "We felt we'd gone beyond that," interjected Vieira.

"The ironing board had been on the '67 through '69 models," Porter remembered (the ironing board was a raised section in the centre of the hood). "We didn't want it so I figured we had too much work in the studio and we had to put the Firebird in the basement studio, way in the bowels of the earth. It was at least a quarter mile from any place (laughter) and I figured if it was down there nobody would notice I was not putting the ironing board on. Mitchell wouldn't walk that far ... and he didn't."

To ensure the ironing board would never appear, Porter enlisted the aid of Bill Collins, assistant chief engineer for the division, who said Pontiac couldn't afford both the ironing board on some models and a different hood for the Trans Am. Collins told Mitchell, who reluctantly concurred there should be no ironing board effect; which delighted Porter and his team no end. Then came the proposed body colour center grille/ bumper. Wayne Vieira was much in favour of the Endura bumper: "We were able to do something nobody else was doing and that was to have the whole bumper in body colour. The rest of the industry were still using chrome bumpers. We had what we called the Endura bumper."

"Oh! That was another one. Another scrape with Mitchell," exclaimed a smiling Porter. "He insisted that the car had to have some chrome bumpers on it. Bumperettes. He said: 'Nobody wants this plastic stuff. It looks cheap and nobody'll like it, so put some chrome on there'.

"We finally came up with some bumperettes, those little outer chrome pieces. In fact the SS Camaro finally wound up with that

Massive 455 HO V-8 was Trans Am's only engine since 1971 when it pumped out 305 bhp net. Two 455 engines were offered in 73; standard was detuned to 250 bhp but there was a 455 SD (Super Duty) rated at 310 bhp later in the year

arrangement, where it had little chrome bumperettes underneath the headlamps. Our design had the Endura front, and the bumperettes just didn't look good."

"Fortunately," continued Porter, "cost considerations again reared its head. Pontiac said it couldn't afford the Endura and the chrome too. Once again we called upon the services of Bill Collins to dissuade Mitchell away from what was basically a bad idea. You see, Mitchell had a corny streak in his make up. He was a brilliant man in so many ways yet he had this vulgar, corny streak in his taste that would suddenly hop out in the most awful ways. And yet he was a brilliant man. He had certain kinds of big views on things that were wonderful, and would fight for what he thought was right. He really was a fearless, courageous fighter.

"He was also capable of being just deadly. He was famous for his bad language and he would say things to you that you wouldn't believe.

Above
Scoops on front fenders of Trans Am were designed to help reduce underhood pressure and, in conjunction with the front air-dam, lessened front end lift during hard acceleration. Fender scoops became tradition with second generation Trans Ams

Right
1973 was the first year for the big Firebird 'chicken' on the Trans Am hood. Bill Mitchell vetoed it in 1970, but designer John Schinella (he succeeded Bill Porter at the Firebird studio) wanted the big bird, and finally won the day

Especially if you didn't immediately grasp what he wanted."

As Bill Porter said, Mitchell was a brilliant man, a genius in many respects. And like many clever, artistic people, Mitchell could be an extremely difficult man to deal with at the best of times, though everyone will agree that his colourful legacy is peppered with legendary cars such as the '63 Corvette, '63 Buick Riviera, and Pontiac Grand Prix – arguably the best trio of new models ever to come out in one year. But we digress …

One typical battle worthy of mention, is that surrounding the Firebird 'screaming chicken' motif. This is the large, colourful bird that became famous spreadeagled across the hood of the Trans Am. It first appeared on the 1967 Firebird as a small motif ahead of the 'Firebird' script on the front fender. Bill Porter redesigned it as a rear fender side marker light in 1969, and by 1970 it had all but disappeared, save for a fairly large decal ahead of the blue stripe on the hood of the Trans Am – which wasn't quite how Bill Porter originally envisaged it. Vieira and Porter remembered the small bird on the fenders of the '68 and '69 models came, courtesy of Phoenix (Arizona) airport. Apparently, Bill Collins saw a mural of an Indian bird on one of the airport's walls, and sent a postcard of it back to the Pontiac studio. From this came the inspiration for the first motif.

"It had been decided to make up two show cars once the '70 had been developed," began Bill. "We thought a big bird on the hood of the Trans Am would be quite effective. I had laid out this huge bird for the

Above
1976 50th Anniversary Limited Edition lamp bezel with anodized gold finish

Left
Standard engine in the 1976 50th Anniversary Trans Am was the L-78 400 OHV V-8 detuned to 185 bhp net, a loss of 40 hp from 1974. Stronger emissions, catalytic converters with single exhausts counted for most of the loss

Above right
Bill Mitchell suggested to styling chief John Schinella that it might be nice to do a Trans Am in the black and gold colours used on the John Player Special. 2500 were built in '76 Pontiac's 50th birthday

Right
The JPS colours were 'sophisticated' according to Mitchell, and certainly the black and gold made the Trans Am stand out. Gold trim and graphics were everywhere while the delicate taillight surrounds had a satin silver finish

Above left
1977 found the black and gold colour scheme repeated, this time on the Special Edition Trans Am. Note the return to dual headlights set within the grille. T-tops first appeared on the 1976 Anniversary Edition, and continued there-after

Below left
Large rear windows first appeared on 1975 Firebird/Trans Am models and was part of Schinella's design influence. Radial tires were standard by 1977, having been introduced on 1973 cars along with 'Radial Tuned Suspension'

Right
Interior, like exterior of Special Edition, was finished in black and gold. Of interest to enthusiasts are the T-tops. Both Fisher Body and Hurst supplied tops, Hurst in 1976/77, Fisher and Hurst in 1978. Hurst tops were smaller, generally used bright trim while Fisher used black trim

hood and it was all ready to go. 3M made the decals and Herbie Adams was going to put them on the two show cars – one an intense blue, the other a pearlescent white. The blue car would have a white bird and vice-versa.

"The white car was in the paint shop having the decal applied to the hood, when Bill Mitchell suddenly walked in and saw this huge bird. He called me on the phone and, honest to God, I've never heard such language in my life! Even out of him! He had a fit! He used every four letter word you could think of, and then some you'd never heard before. Then he told me the car looked like a Macey's truck!

"'Get this blankety-blankety-blank Macey's truck out of this blankety-blankety-blank paint shop immediately,' he screamed. And that was the end of the bird, right there." As we have already noted, the bird, much diminished in size, turned up on the nose of the '70 Trans Am. Yet in 1973, thanks to the tenacity and faith of John Schinnella, the designer who took over the Firebird studio in 1971, the big bird re-appeared on the place it was always meant to be – the Trans Am hood. Herb Adams and Bill Collins had seen a hemi Shaker scoop on top of either a Plymouth or Dodge muscle car. They were much taken with the scoop and felt it was just what the Trans Am hood needed. In the meantime, Bill Porter had been working on twin scoops for the Formula 400, when he was asked to design a shaker scoop.

"The idea was for the scoop to face backwards," said Porter, "because there was a high pressure area at the base of the windshield that would

cause the air to go into the scoop. However, Pontiac had to share the Camaro windshield which sat further back than on the Firebird prototype, which meant the scoop wouldn't be nearly as effective. "I still favoured the twin scoops which ultimately came out on the Formula 400 located up front. They were truly grab-air scoops located where they were for that reason. Still, Adams and Collins coerced me into designing the rearward facing scoop." (Which came out on the 1970 Trans Am.)

Naturally Bill Mitchell didn't like the scoops. "He didn't like the ones I liked, and he didn't like the ones Collins liked," chuckled Porter. "And when his first Firebird was done for him ... the division would always prep a car for him as his personal toy for a month, maybe a year ... Mitchell specified no scoops even though it had the hottest engine under the hood. Hotter than the general public would ever see." The battles were over, the cars in the showrooms. Motoring journalists generally

Above
An urgent visit to the optician is recommended if you spot a Special Edition Trans Am and can't read the mile high letters at the rear. Large letters only appeared on the Trans Am. Special Editions could be ordered either in gold or black and gold for 1978

Left
Solar gold was the name given to the colour of 1978's Trans Am Special Edition. Car had natty camel tan interior, Fisher or Hurst T-tops. From 1977 buyers could order T-tops for any Firebird model

liked the new models, yet sales slipped to an all time low. Only 48,739 Firebirds and Trans Ams were built, partly because production delays held up introduction until 26 February 1970. But the main reason for lack of sales was public apathy in the face of high insurance rates, increasing government regulations and Vietnam. Nobody was sure anymore; the times were a-changin' and it didn't look good.

Dummy fender louvers, Bill Porter-designed honeycomb wheels, and the 455 cubic inch V-8 were the positive sides to the 1971 Firebird. With the government and insurance companies breathing down its corporate neck, GM lowered compression ratios in all its engines to no higher than 8.5:1. This would allow the use of regular, low lead fuel even in the mightiest engines. Horsepower was down, too. The base six dropped ten to 145, and the highest figure for the 400 was 300 hp. Although these figures are for gross horsepower, the motor industry switched to net horsepower in 1971. All further figures will be described in net horsepower figures.

Although only 2,116 Trans Ams were built, it was the Firebird flagship. One couldn't mistake it in a shopping mall car park or on the open road. It looked different: it was different. Under the hood resided the 455 putting out 335 gross hp. Unique to the Trans Am were all the spoilers. Front ones, rear ones and side ones. Perhaps the Trans Am did look a little like an over-dressed duchess, but those spoilers made all the difference to the car's handling. According to Bill Porter, the spoilers came from the Camaro group. Chevrolet had allowed the designers to take a Camaro down to Marietta, Georgia, to the Lockheed wind tunnel for aerodynamic tests. Tests were carried out, with and without spoilers. Steve Malone at Pontiac didn't think the tests were necessary – those were the days when aerodynamics weren't considered very important.

Chevrolet's tests yielded a lot of information which eventually ended up in the Camaro studio under Henry Haga. But the information was put into a file and forgotten. Porter thinks Chevrolet didn't want to spend the money on spoilers whereas he knew they were what was needed for the Trans Am.

"One of the big problems on the Trans Am," said Porter, "was down-force, because it had all this torque and horsepower. It wasn't so much a question of reducing drag; with 400/455 cubic inch engines you could virtually ram the thing through the air. It was a question of keeping the car on the ground. We didn't want it to fly!" Enlisting the help of gifted young engineer, Doug Patterson, who worked in conjunction with both

Many dream of cruising the lonely, sunny roads of Arizona in a car as nice as the 1978 Special Edition Trans Am, pictured here. 6.6 litre engine was standard with a four-speed manual transmission though most buyers specified automatic

the Firebird and Camaro studios, Porter felt it would be justified to obtain a copy of the tests. Fortunately Patterson thought likewise; he didn't want to see these valuable tests go to waste, so he got the information and gave it to Porter. "He (Patterson) kind of bootlegged a copy of that Camaro study," grinned Porter. "It had all the data we needed; exactly how big the spoilers should be, where they should be. Don't forget, the Camaro and Firebird have essentially the same body.

"All those spoilers on the Trans Am", continued Porter, "were built to the specifications from the Camaro wind-tunnel work. We religiously followed them. Once we built the spoilers and put it altogether, the Trans Am was dramatically improved aerodynamically.

"It wasn't long after that Chevrolet engineers found out their wind tunnel tests were responsible for the Trans Am's ground effects. Understandably they were none too happy. Bill Collins had pangs of

Late afternoon western sun plays across '78 Special Edition dashboard, which possesses traditional round instruments set in a pseudo machined turned panel. Cover is often used in Arizona and western states to protect plastic dashboards from sun

Gold anodized grille inserts distinguished the 1978 Special Edition Trans Am from the rest. 8,600 Gold specials were made, of which 1,600 were equipped with a four-speed manual transmission; 1978 cars so equipped are the rarest of all 1970s T/A Special Editions.

remorse, so he let Chevrolet have the deck-lid portion of the spoilers. Pontiac had already paid for the tooling, quite a considerable expense, so the two divisions made peace with each other after the smoke cleared. Incidentally, the spoilers first appeared on the 1970 Trans Am.

As we have already seen, the year that sales reached their lowest level during the Firebird's short history, was 1970. Of those sales, only one in five left the factory as a Formula 400 or Trans Am. Though nothing to really write home about, production moved up a little in 1971 to 53,124. But 1972 production figures were so bad it's quite suprising that Pontiac didn't pull the plug on the Firebird. 29,951 units was a very small total by American standards.

Although the turmoil of the sixties had become little more than a bad taste in politicians' mouths, the affects of the on-going Vietnam war, the aftermath of the youth revolution and, nearer to home, the threat of oil

shortages coupled with a motor industry under duress, served to find Americans not quite so sure of their identity anymore. This insecurity was much in evidence in Detroit during the seventies where the car makers, harassed by Federal regulations, caught the malaise and created arguably the worst and most unimaginative automobiles America had ever seen. Then along came the all-conquering Japanese – but that is another story.

Even though the seventies produced cars that should never have been made, there were lights in the tunnel. One, of course, was the Firebird. Then there was Camaro. Both Pontiac and Chevrolet wisely decided against any new models, keeping the same body until the early eighties. Pontiac's 1972 Firebirds were virtually unchanged from the previous year. There was a honeycomb mesh in the grille that reflected Bill Porter's honeycomb wheels. Net horsepower ratings became an industry standard. Now the 455 V8 developed 300 hp net, the 400 was rated at 250. The six developed 110 hp. The two-speed automatic was still being offered but was finally laid to rest halfway through the year. Thereafter, all models offered only GM's world class Turbo Hydra-Matic.

Pontiac was beset by problems in 1972, all of them relating to the Firebird. GM management wanted to administer the *coup de grace* to the ponycar whose sales had been disappointing to say the least. And 1972 was on course for the worst Firebird production figures yet. Hurried meetings, boardroom barneys and high stress factors became the order of the day. Then, to really put the cat among the pigeons, the United Auto Workers union decided to have a crippling 174-day long strike at the one plant building Firebirds and Camaros, in Norwood, Ohio. Millions of dollars and thousands of cars were lost. When it finally ended in September, Pontiac were forced to destroy several hundred cars because there had not been time to implement 1973 safety standards. Still, the wrangling over whether the Firebird should be dropped was resolved in Pontiac's favour. The pony had won a reprieve.

Above
An interesting special was the all-blue Skybird. Based on the luxury Esprit Firebird, the Skybird started off as a pre-production showcar called the Bluebird. Reaction to the Bluebird was strong enough to put it into production

Right
Like Harley-Davidsons and Cadillacs, the Pontiac Firebird is an automotive icon worthy of miniature reproduction. Catch 'em young

At the end of 1971, Bill Porter was promoted, and his place was taken by John Schinella. Schinella was a gifted young designer who soon put his mark on the Firebird when he decided to resurrect the 'screaming chicken' hood motif so angrily dismissed by Bill Mitchell. Schinella revived Bill Porter's original idea, redesigned it, and talked Bill Mitchell into allowing it on the 1973 Trans Am hood. Which surprisingly he did. At a time when the Trans Am was virtually all that was left with halfway decent performance, the chicken was a great image booster.

Under the hood, Pontiac let it be known that the Trans Am had no intention of becoming another anaemic also-ran with the inclusion of the Super Duty 455 as a spirited option. Horsepower was rated at 290; the other 455 developed 250. 1973 Firebirds had a choice of seven engines in various states of tune, but all with reduced power. An egg-crate grille replaced the honeycomb of the previous year.

Though they wouldn't say it publicly, America's politicians knew Vietnam was a horrible mistake and were desperately trying to extricate themselves from a mire of their own making. Unfortunately, the consequences of the war were far reaching – it split a nation in two, and it would take much more than super glue to repair the damage which, at best, was a loss of direction. The OPEC countries then seized their chance with an oil embargo in protest against America's support of Israel. Oil, the lifeline of the nation, suffered huge price increases and the threat of gas rationing. A 55 mph speed limit was imposed across the country, and the motor industry came under increasing pressure to build smaller, more economical cars. On top of all that, there was Watergate.

Never before had a motor industry faced so many problems all at once. Most of its efforts were directed at having to satisfy the government, who had stipulated ridiculous time limits to carry the Federal measures out. Judging by the dreadful cars that were built during the seventies, the designers had lost their sense of direction, as had the nation. Pontiac's troubles were as acute as the rest of the industry's. Uninspired designs prevailed – I mean, who would rave about a Ventura or a Phoenix? At least the 1973 Grand Am showed all was not lost, for it really was a stylish car with performance to match. As for the Firebird – it was Pontiac's mascot, its image maker, that little oasis of sunshine no amount of Federal edicts could put asunder. The designers knew it: they loved it, and kept it on course to survive those bad, bad days.

Innovation was the keynote to John Schinella's considerable front and rear facelift on the Firebird/Trans Am. The Pontiac design team took the

Esprit Skybird had cast aluminum snowflake wheels painted blue, blue Custom interior, a blue Trans Am steering wheel, blue seatbelts, blue T-tops ... in fact, everything was blue. A special Skybird decal was created for the sail panels

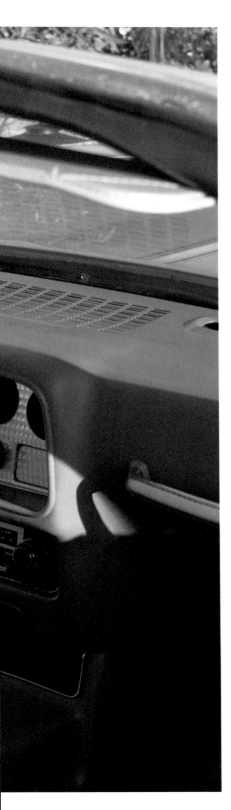

Endura soft nose theme on the earlier cars, and turned it into a complete front and rear cap. In other words, a complete section comprising grille, lamp openings and bumper that 'snapped' into place over the front sheet metal without changing anything else; the same at the rear except for some to the lower rear fenders and tail panel to accommodate the wraparound software. Given that the car's body was hardly touched, the new front and rear made the Firebird look like an entirely different car. The twin grilles were narrower and slanted forward, shovel-nose style. Thick black rubber bumpers were added front and rear: Schinella said they really weren't needed, but were incorporated to get the public used to the urethane moldings.

Unlike most of the industry's first crude attempts at 5 mph bumpers, the Firebird's were cleverly integrated beneath the plastic nose and tail. Heavy horizontal steel bars were attached to a pair of telescopic shocks.

Above
Replacing the polycast honeycomb wheels of 1971–1976 were the cast aluminum snowflake variety which came about in 1977. There were three different varieties; the one shown is the 8 in. which came with the WS-6 handling package

Left
Carmine red trim, gold dashboard, doeskin vinyl upholstery, and red T/A steering wheel make up the interior of the 1978 Skybird successor, the Redbird. The Redbird was an option package (W.68) for the luxury Esprit model, and cost $430-$465

If the car was thumped in the back or front at speeds up of to 5 mph, the shocks automatically telescoped, then bouncing back after the impact. Simple, yes, but it worked. There were the usual four engines but available in eight different rates of tune. Standard engine for the Trans Am was the 400 rated at 225 hp. The 455 Superduty V-8 became an option, and developed 290 hp. Variable ratio became standard across the Firebird range.

After the hellish 1972 sales figures, the only way Firebird could go was up. Which it did in 1973, production almost doubling to 46.313 units, of which 4,802 were Trans Ams. Then in 1974, at a time when the price of gas was at a premium, a total of 73,729 Firebirds were built, including a whopping 10,255 Trans Ams. No accounting for the moods of the general public, that's for sure. In a road test of a '74 Firebird Esprit, equipped with a 400 cubic inch, 175 hp V-8, critics got an incredible 19.2

The bottom of Skybird, below the bumper, was painted a darker blue than the rest of the car. Seven engines were available, from Buick's 231 cid V6 to Oldsmobile's 403 V8. The Buick engine replaced Chevrolet's in-line six used since 1970

Darker blue was also used for Skybird taillight bezels; in fact the rear end looks very restrained and quite handsome. Paint code for those who might have a Skybird that needs restoring is Code 21

mpg, reasonable, if not wonderful, road holding – don't forget this was the boulevard cruising Firebird – but had its doors blown off by a Dodge Challenger sporting a 318 cubic inch V-8 in both acceleration and quarter mile runs. Mind you, the Esprit weighed almost 300 lbs more than the Challenger, which might explain the disparity.

Production climbed again in 1975 to 84,063. In 1976 it went to 110,775. Possibly the reason for the dramatic increases was that the Javelin, Challenger and Barracuda had all bitten the dust, that the Mustang II was a ponycar in name only, and Firebird's only rival was its cousin, the Camaro. From 1975, all Firebirds had 15 in. wheels shod in radial tires, built to GM specifications. Speedometers had kilometers as well as mph, in anticipation of America switching to the metric system. Pontiac, and all other motor manufacturers are still, anticipating …

The most recognizable change was the wraparound rear window.

Firebird designers had wanted to add the larger window for years, and would have done so in the sixties had it not been for cost considerations. From 1975 on, the wraparound glass became a permanent fixture on all Firebirds bar convertibles. As for engines, in face of the increasing pressure for better gas mileage, the 455 Super Duty was dropped, albeit only temporarily. The 400 was now the Trans Am's biggest block. Rated at only 185 hp it appeared the Trans Am's days were numbered.

Pontiac didn't want to follow in Chevrolet's footsteps. Chevrolet had dropped the Z-28, leaving the Trans Am as the only super ponycar left. The image, though, was being compromised. Meetings took place and in the end, then Pontiac general manager, Martin Caserio, ordered the 455 back into production but with a four-speed manual as the only transmission. There was little doubt that the Firebird meant a lot to its designers and engineers. Their enthusiasm built a car that was certainly better than most. Its image soon caught the attention of Hollywood directors. Remember, James Garner always drove a Firebird in the long running *Rockford Files* TV series. Rockford was shown all over the world and helped introduce the Firebird to motoring buffs in many countries. In the U.S., quite a few sales were made as a result of the exposure on Rockford. So who says TV programmes are not influential?

In the mid- to late-seventies, the Firebird's brawny but svelte image was given a further boost when Burt Reynolds drove Trans Ams in *Hooper* and *Smoky and the Bandit*. People liked what they saw on the silver screen and it wasn't long before Firebirds made their way to Britain, Europe and Australia. General Motors Europe puts together several of its American cars in an assembly plant that the company runs in Antwerp, Belgium. Here, cars such as the Chevrolet Caprice are assembled to European specifications for European customers. There is a strong possibility that six-cylinder Firebirds with stiffer suspension may also have been built in very small numbers at Antwerp. You would soon know — the speedometer would be in kilometers only.

Changes in 1976 consisted of the removal of the black rubber bumper strips, parking lights taken from the grilles and placed beneath the bumper. The front bumper area was more rectangular and the rear was considerably changed. T-tops became an option for the first time and the Formula Firebird was given its own identity with its name emblazoned in large graphics along the door bottoms; there were no changes mechanically. The Formula still had twin scoops, the Trans Am

Here one can clearly see the Skybird insignia on the roof pillar; it looks as though it was inspired by 19th-century Chinese art. Paint has dulled a little on the door — a quite common problem with many cars during the seventies

the ever-popular shaker scoop nestling between the large, flattened bird.

1976 also saw the first of many 'Special Edition' Firebirds. This one was a black and gold Trans Am with a gold bird on the hood. The car was built to celebrate Pontiac's 50th anniversary. Production problems limited the Hurst-designed T-tops to a mere 647 units – the Special Edition models were all supposed to have T-tops. A further 1,947 cars were assembled with normal roofs.

Interiors of all Firebirds were an American's idea of how a sports car interior should be. There was little, if any, resemblance to European or British sports car interiors which were never as comfortable or as convenient as the American ones. Rich looking Madrid Morrokide vinyl upholstered the seating areas, the dashboard sported a set of legible, round instruments, and the shift lever sat in a center console. Front seating was comfortable, especially in the Esprit, but rear passengers would have had a hard time of it in the Firebird's first decade. This is true of any 2+2, regardless of make.

People had come to terms with higher gas prices, and the 55 mph speed limit which was being challenged on a daily basis by drivers equipped with a new plaything. The radar detector had come into being and was no doubt purchased by the majority of Firebird/Trans Am owners. By 1977 the Firebird was beginning to show its age after seven years with the same body. To rejuvenate the car, John Schinella designed a more aggressive look for the front end. The split grilles received rectangular quad headlights, each grille turning down sharply at the centre to form a pronounced Vee. Schinella had been inspired by the angry looking eyebrows of one of the coaches for the Detroit Lions. Talk about one's looks being immortalized on a car front!

A decklid spoiler was standard on the Formula which had become a Trans Am without the big bird. Buick's new 105 hp V-6 replaced the Chevy straight six engine as standard fare. A new Pontiac-built 301 V-8 made its debut, a 403 developing 185 hp replaced the 455, and the 400 continued, as did the good old 350.

Perhaps the sharpest looking set of wheels ever to come out of Detroit appeared for the first time on the Firebird series. They were shaped like a snowflake seen through a magnifying glass. These wheels also appeared on other Pontiacs and are very desirable today.

Another special edition was trotted out – this time the Esprit Skybird, which had started out as a show car called the Blue Bird. It attracted much attention and was put into production as the Skybird package;

Here's another one of several British owned Firebirds that appear in this book – gives it an international flavour, don't you think? First Formula appeared as a 1970 model and has continued ever since. Car shown is somewhat modified '77/78 model

Pontiac couldn't use the Blue Bird name, as someone else held the copyright. The Skybird was painted two-tone blue; the upper portion was light blue, the bottom, dark blue. Aluminum snowflake wheels, light to dark blue canopy stripes, a blue interior, and blue grilles actually made the car quite attractive. All it needed was Little Boy Blue to step out from behind the wheel!

Production shot up yet again, this time to 155,736. The most popular model was the Trans Am, with 68,745 produced. So much for 55 mph and expensive gas; Americans were determined to have some fun out of life and no OPEC oil country was going to tell them how to live. No, sir!

A new appearance package surfaced in 1978; this time it was the Redbird, which replaced the Skybird. As the Skybird had been blue, the Redbird theme was, well, red. A gold Special Edition Trans Am popped up mid-year, and there was still the black and gold one. In the engine department, the 301 disappeared to be replaced by a 305 cubic inch V-8 rated at 145 hp. Chevrolet's 350 replaced Pontiac's own, and the stage was being set for the use of corporate engines. Otherwise nothing had changed.

Trans Am production for 1978 soared to 93,341, while overall production climbed to 187,285. And if you think that's pretty good, look at 1979's totals: 211,454 of which 117,109 were Trans Ams. Ten years earlier, only 697 Trans Ams had been built; dedication built the Trans Am, and that dedication had paid off.

Once again there was a facelift. Although work was already progressing on the third generation replacement, the new car wouldn't debut until 1982, so Schinella's team had to keep the old body looking as fresh as possible. The rectangular quad lights were separated on either side into recessed pods, the centre section became a pronounced beak, and the twin grilles became, in essence, the bumpers. At the rear, the taillights were set into a full width black plastic lens which, when lit, or the brakes were applied – four wheel disc brakes became an option on Trans Ams and Formulas – the lenses shone red.

More engine fiddling found the 301 cid V-8 reinstated in two horse-power modes; 140 and 150. The 305 dropped from 145 to 133 hp, but the 400 climbed to 220. The Oldsmobile-built 403 was still 185 hp. This would be the last year for the true big block motors of old, and they were soon to be put out to grass.

An interesting Trans Am was the limited edition Tenth Anniversary

Here's a Trans Am with a difference! Its colour scheme and bird decal are unique to this car. This is a 1978 model and has the W-72 high performance package identified by the 'T/A 6.6' on the hood shaker

model. Painted silver and charcoal, the Trans Am had silver roof hatches, silver leather seats, silver door panels — silver wherever it could go. Under the hood was the 400 cubic inch V-8, now referred to as a 6.6 litre as Detroit turned to metric. 7500 of this somewhat decadent model were produced.

There were virtually no changes in the 1980/81 Firebirds, but there were a few Special Editions. The Esprit Redbird gave way to the Esprit Yellowbird, yes, yellow everything. A Trans Am was chosen to pace the Daytona 500 so a silver replica was built in limited numbers. Another was the Indianapolis 500 Pace Car sporting Trans Am's first turbo-charged engine, a 301 (4.9 litre) developing 210 hp.

Since the Iranian revolution in 1979, another gas crisis had loomed. Pontiac decided long before that big engines were redundant, and the way ahead was smaller, fuel efficient units. Ergo, the largest engine in the '80/81 Firebird line-up was the 305 (5.0 litres). Buick's venerable V-6 remained as standard.

In spite of a decade that didn't exactly help America's image around the globe — the Watergate scandal resulting in Nixon resigning rather than face impeachment, the ignominious, though much welcomed, end to the Vietnam war — Pontiac, at least, could pat itself on the back by proving to the doubters there was still room for exciting cars like the Firebird.

From the heady heights of the year before, 1980 production sagged to 107,340 while Trans Am sales, despite the specials, dropped by over a half against the previous year. It was a dramatic year in which John Lennon was shot, Ronald Reagan was elected President and changes were about to take place in the good old U.S. of A. By 1981, with an unchanged car, Firebird production was down to under 71,000. Everybody was waiting for the brand new, third generation model which was to be introduced in January 1982.

A new era was about to begin.

Above right
Two-tone yellow paint and orange striping are striking to behold. Paint, stripes and hood bird are the only modifications on an otherwise factory-original car. Paintwork is well done and actually suits Trans Am lines

Below right
Even at night the specially painted Trans Am looks good. In fact, the pearlescent yellow body sides and trunk really stand out. Not only does Randy and Tina Gobbels' car stand out, but it is loaded with almost everything Pontiac could put on it

The Times,
They are A-Changin'

Bob Dylan

There was a new message blowing across the land. It spoke of pride, of confidence in oneself, of self help. It would instill a sense of purpose lost during the past two decades. But, as Americans eventually found out, the cost would be more than the nation could bear. Even the car industry became a victim towards the end of the eighties. One of those recessions that tend to pop up with depressing regularity every ten years or so in capitalist societies, gripped America by the throat in the early eighties. By the time that the third generation Firebird made its debut in January 1982, the recession had almost spent itself.

Work had begun on the new Firebird in 1975, after Pontiac and Camaro had argued the advantages of keeping the front engine, rear-drive layout instead of sharing one of GM's front-drive platforms which had been proposed as an economical alternative. The F-Body won the day, and work began in earnest. "After I left Pontiac I went to the advanced design studios," began Bill Porter, "and spent a number of years there. It was here that I had a role in developing the third generation car. My assistant at that time was a fellow named Roger Huett, and I would credit Roger with much of the design as well.

"There was a McLaren race car of the early to mid-seventies that we liked the looks of, and when we started work on the '82 Firebird we were very much influenced by it. I think it was the McLaren ... I'll have to look it up. Anyway, a year or two later an aerodynamic Ferrari came out; I'm trying to think who designed it. I think it was Bertone but it may have been Ghia. It had a windshield that was concave, sort of bell-shaped, at the base. It was unheard of at the time, to blend a convex top with a concave base.

"We incorporated this windshield affect into the lines of the earlier race car. This hybrid was the start of a series of designs that ultimately became the basis for the '82 Firebird."

Redbird replaced 1977 Skybird in 1978, and was continued in 1979 with a dramatic new face. Split grilles, or apetures, were set lower to give even more aggressive look. John Schinella says he wanted hidden headlights, but cost prohibited them

After the advanced studio's initial design work, the car, after a few fits and starts, became Pontiac Chief Stylist, John Schinella's project. The car had to be smaller while still keeping the same interior space of the second generation Firebird. In a real about-face, Schinella dumped the aggressive, macho look of old. What resulted was a smooth, aerodynamic shape with a drag co-efficient of 0.33 for the Firebird, 0.32 for the Trans Am. Underneath the sophisticated looking exterior the front engine, rear-drive format had been much modified to be almost unrecognizable. The wishbone front suspension had given way to a MacPherson-type using front struts with inboard mounted coil springs. At the rear, the old 'cartwheel' leaf springs were finally banished to be replaced by coils and a pair of trailing links to keep the live axle in place.

Bearing in mind the quest for economical operation, Pontiac dispensed with the traditional big blocks to lay rubber, choosing instead

Above
Detail of snowflake wheel shows red paint, polished cast aluminum spokes. Wheel had slightly different pattern to 1977 version, and weighed less. Bird in hub had red outer feathers on Redbird package. Gregg Anderer is the second owner

Left
Gold anodized dashboard, Carmine red doeskin upholstery (it wasn't really doeskin, it was simply a name that sounded better than just plain vinyl), red T/A steering wheel, red carpets, red everything – this was the interior that graced the 1979 Redbird

to deliver power with smaller engines, the smallest being Chevrolet's four-cylinder 'Iron Duke' rated at 90 hp. This was the Firebird's base engine and, while not particularly powerful, it was at least economical – quite environmentally and reasonably insurance friendly.

Chevrolet's 2.8 V-6 developed 102 hp and took over from the larger Buick six. As for V-8s there were two: a 145 hp 5.0 litre with a 4-bbl Quadrajet, and a 165 horse version of the same block with Corvette's 'Crossfire' fuel-injection system. This was the Trans Am's mightiest engine yet with 0–60 times taking nine seconds, people began to wonder whether there really was no substitute for cubic inches. There was one snag: none of the new engines were built by Pontiac. This was not the sort of news Firebird enthusiasts wanted to hear. Many felt cheated. They had managed to live with the fact that Camaro and Firebird shared the same body, but were comforted with the knowledge that the engines

Above

Script above headlights ensures everybody knows that this particular Esprit is the Redbird. Owner Greg Anderer remembers his neighbors buying the car when he was eleven. He was so enamoured by it he decided he would have to have the car one day

Right

The maze of pipes and emissions almost hide 301 V8 from view. Engine was dropped in favour of Chevy's 305 in 1978, then reinstated in 1979. 301 was quite potent, gave good gas mileage and 120 mph was the top speed

were Pontiac's own. Now they learn both cars shared Chevrolet's 5.0 litre engine (henceforth to be known as a GM unit), a cost-cutting measure supposedly to minimise wasteful repetition. Individuality was to be a thing of the past; there would be corporate engines, corporate bodies, and a very corporate identity in the future. If this seems like a touch of the old déjà vu, it is if one remembers British Leyland.

15 x 7 in. wheels, 10.5 in. disc brakes all round, and quicker (2.5 turns lock to lock) recirculating ball steering, complete the main picture. A $600 optional handling package (WS6) consisted of some of the above, and limited slip differential, Goodyear Eagle radial tires, and heavier suspension parts. With all this, handling was fairly predictable so long as the roads were smooth, straight, and dry, although there wasn't much to compare with the previous models.

Three models made the new line-up; a base Firebird with the four-cylinder engine, the Firebird SE, and the Trans Am. Instead there was a return to the 'ironing board' bulge, a design feature Bill Porter deplored on the '67 to '69 Firebirds. Instead of extending the whole hood length as on the earlier cars, the bulge was to the left of the centre line, finishing halfway along the hood. It did have a functional purpose though, as it was a rearward facing scoop grabbing air from the base of the windshield. Directional lamps were hidden behind what looked like horizontal arrow slits, and single headlights retracted flush with the hood. Pontiac's traditional twin grilles covered the parking lamps, and were set into the integrated, bumper-cum-spoiler. In common with the Camaro, the car was designated a hatchback coupé due to the decklid and large rear window opening as a single unit. The hatchback design was a first for the F-bodied pony cars resulting in a little more room for golf clubs.

Even though GM was without direction, Pontiac acutely so in the early eighties, the new Firebird produced 116,362 units, of which Trans Am was the largest selling model. This was a considerable increase over 1981's total, thus confirming the suspicion that buyers were awaiting the new model. By 1982 the energy crisis was all but over, thanks to responsible conservation policies enacted by the industrialised west. The result was a huge oil glut and tumbling gas prices. Sighs of relief were expressed by the motor industry; over at Pontiac there were thoughts of bringing back some real muscle to the Firebird.

Changes to the Firebird line were relatively mild over the next few years. Long gone were the days of annual change; quite simply, the

Gregg Anderer finally realised his dream; his years of cleaning and waxing his neighbour's Redbird had not been in vain, for they sold it to him when he was old enough to drive. Low angle shot shows how grilles were part of bumper

money wasn't there for such extravagance any more. Instead, a new model evolves and improves over the years until it can be improved no longer. Sailing under a catchy 'We Build Excitement' banner from 1983, Pontiac began to direct its energies in divorcing itself from the look-alikes fielded by GM's other divisions, and giving the Firebird back its own unique brand of excitement. First came a Special Edition commemorating the 25th Daytona 500, of which only 2500 were built. This model had special paint, Recaro leather upholstery, a 5.0 litre GM V-8, and cast aluminum wheels. Another special was a black and gold Recaro Trans Am with fully adjustable Recaro leather seats. And much to the driving enthusiast's delight, both the Trans Am and S/E models had a five-speed manual transmission as standard.

Production slumped to 74,884 units, of which 31,930 were Trans Ams. In 1984 production climbed again to 128,304, the highest it had

Above
Besides the front, Schinella and his team changed the rear as well. Black opaque strips extend side to side over taillight lenses. When lit, the lights shone red through the strips. This 1979 Trans Am was photographed at Knebworth in Herts, England.

Right
Finding one of these on a walk through English parklands is unlikely – but they are there, and in growing numbers. 'T/A 6.6' on the scoop shows car has 220 bhp engine. Four-wheel disc brakes were offered for first time on Formula and T/A models in 1979

been since 1979. As for the '84 models, there was little to distinguish them from the previous year, except the Trans Am offered a new aero package consisting of muscular spoilers and wings. An oddity was the dropping of the fuel-injected V-8 and replacing it with a carbureted version of the same thing, but tweaked to 190 hp. After years of low compression ratios, the new engine was 9.5:1, quite a sizeable jump.

By 1987 Pontiac was on a roll. Everything the division built was good. Hi-tech sedans were approaching BMW standards; in fact several U.S. car magazines referred to Pontiac as the 'American Bimmer'. Many praised the advanced little Fiero first introduced in 1984. There was nothing else on the market quite like it.

On the Firebird front, there were important changes for '87. There was a new Trans Am model, the GTA; another was the latest Formula. The base Firebird carried this package. A tuned port fuel injected 5.0

Here is a Trans Am sans the big 'chicken' (it was always an option and a fairly expensive one at that) attending Britain's major American car event, the pre-'50 American Auto Club's Rally of the Giants that takes place early in July at Knebworth House, Knebworth, Herts

1979 was the Trans Am's tenth anniversary, so John Schinella suggested the idea of a special anniversary model to Pontiac general manager Alex Mair. Mair concurred, and here is one of the 7500 consecutively numbered Tenth Anniversary Editions

litre V-8 developing 205 hp was optional, the 4 bbl 5.0 litre with 165 hp standard. As for the GTA, well, that came with the big 5.7 litre fuel-injected, 210 horse Corvette V-8 as standard, while the stock Trans Am started off with the 165 hp 4 bbl 5.0 litre mill. A fresh, more rounded front and rear helped keep the new Firebird slipperier through the air, thus enhancing its already good drag co-efficient. The hood of the Trans Am GTA had twin scoops at the front, and a pair on each side at the rear. The Formula favoured the rear facing 'ironing board' duct. A 140 mph speedometer spoke of a car that was able to travel at a high rate of knots – *Motor Trend* recorded a top speed in excess of 141 mph!

Consumer Guide's 'Auto '87' annual car review wasn't too complimentary about the GTA's ride which they said "took smooth, dry roads to enjoy the high handling limits because rough pavement will leave lasting impressions on the driver and passengers ... " In other words, the

suspension was too stiff. Still, for a road car costing close to $20,000 and weighing almost 3500 lbs, the GTA was extremely good. Standard wheel size on base Firebirds was 15 in. but there was a 16 x 8.0 cast alloy wheel shod in fat P245/50VR16 tires. These helped handling immeasurably. Another option most people 'in the know' specified was the WS6 handling package. For $385, the buyer got the aforementioned wheels and tires, 36mm front and 24mm rear anti-roll bars, specially tuned springs, gas filled shock absorbers, and quick ratio power steering. This was available as part of a larger option package costing $1070 on the Formula. "Pontiac fires off a turbocharged 20th Anniversary salute to horsepower fans everywhere." So began a special Trans Am brochure celebrating yet another Special Edition car, this time the 20th Anniversary Trans Am which also happened to be the official Indy 500 Pace Car. Only 1500 of this model would be built. Instant profitability – for greedy speculators, naturally.

True hi-tech power guided the Indy Trans Am. Under the hood lay a 250 hp turbo-charged V-6 with a massive 340 lbs/ft of torque. The engine, which came from Buick's short-lived Grand National and GNX muscle cars, was modified by Pontiac and a performance concern called PAS Inc. for inclusion in the special GTA. With this engine, it was claimed by independent testers to be able to top 160 mph and take a mere five seconds to go from 0–60. This meant that the car was faster than a V-8 powered Corvette! And certainly faster than the 5.7 litre, V-8 powered GTA or Formula. A Firebird coupe joined the fray in 1989. The base engine was the 2.8 litre fuel injected V-6, the 4 banger consigned to limbo. The cheapest Firebird cost $11,999, the most expensive – the GTA – $20,339. The former was pretty basic, the latter loaded. With the huge range of options and packages available, some people preferred to opt for the cheaper car, and option it out the way they wanted it.

Work had already begun on the fourth generation Firebirds well before the final facelift of the 1982 design. That came early in 1991, and it gave the ageing body an entirely fresh look. Inspired by the Banshee show car of a few seasons before, the soft, rounded front with its two slots covering parking lights and turn signals, conjured up visions of a tadpole; it had the embryonic look of a larval frog. The Trans Am GTA did, anyway. Both the Formula and Trans Am weren't quite so tadpole-looking, as their fronts sported grille openings coming to a point at the center. An integrated rear spoiler, new bodyside skirting, and new taillights all served to enhance the dramatic design. Under the hood,

For $10,619.55, the 10th anniversary T/A had it all, and more. Schinella-designed Turbo-Alloy, 15x8 wheels, two-tone silver paint, silver leather upholstery, a bird crest embroidered on seats and door panels, WS-6 handling package ... and the list goes on

engines began with the 3.1 V-6 developing 140 hp and standard with the base Firebird. This particular engine replaced the old 2.8 litre six. Next came a pair of 5.0 litre V-8s, one with port fuel injection, the other with throttle body injection. The former developed 225 hp, the latter 170. Biggest engine of all was the perennial 5.7 litre V-8 that pumped out 240 hp. It was the largest production V-8 powering a passenger car. Perhaps the most welcome news for wind-in-your-hair motoring fans, was the return of a convertible to the Firebird line after an absence of 20 years. This came with either the 5.0 or 5.7 litre fuel injected V-8s.

Planet Earth had changed. Changes had occurred that nobody ever thought they would live to see. The Soviet Union was no more; Communism had died at the doorway to Lenin's tomb. All eastern Europe – Hungary, Poland, Czechoslovakia among them – were free, democratic nations once again. The turnabout was sudden, catching the free world by surprise. The change was so complete that a 1991 map of the world looked very similar to the map of 1891. The possibilities for trade with East Europe was tremendous, a fact that didn't go unheeded in Detroit's corridors of power. Perhaps the day is not far off when Russians will be tooling around Moscow in a Trans Am!

While these historic changes were taking place, the West was at the beginning of one of the worst recessions to hit for many years. Its ferocity led to it being compared to the Great Depression. Firebird production spiralled downwards from 110,463 in 1986 to 20,553 in 1990. There was a pickup due to the facelift in 1991 (50,234 produced),

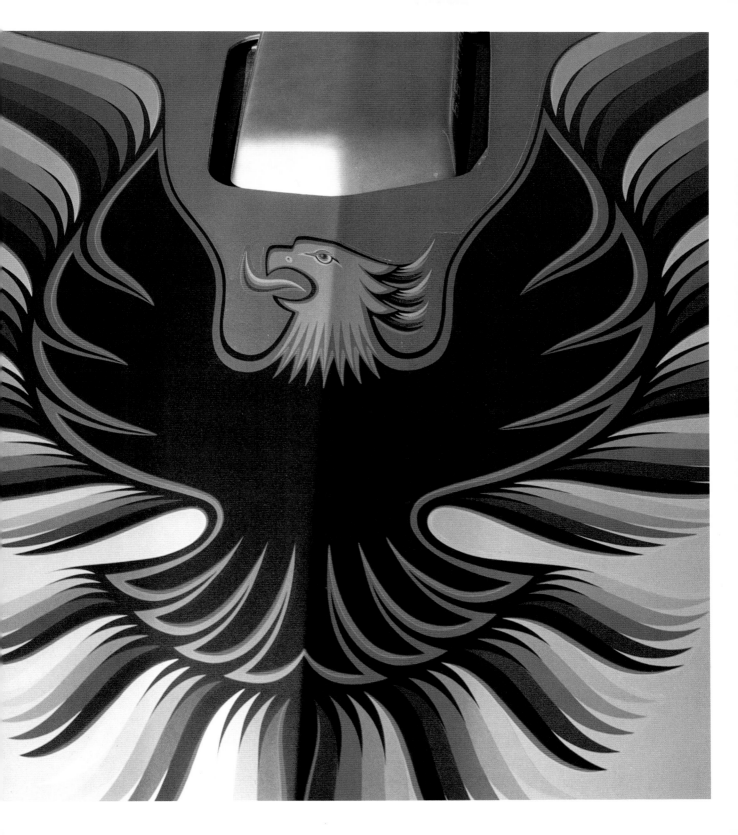

but the impetus wained; only 27,567 left the factories in 1992, the final year for the third generation Firebird. Not that one would think this was the case, reading a Pontiac brochure describing the 1992 models thus: "In an age of here-today-gone-tomorrow automotive fashion", begins the text alongside a dashing Trans Am convertible populated by a pair of beautiful people, "the Firebird is an enduring link to everything that has made Pontiacs legends in their own time. With the largest V-8 available in a production automobile, the solid feel of rear-wheel drive, and a profile that is yet to age, Pontiac Firebird is as bold and timeless as a car can get. That, friends, is what we call an attitude." Wow!! Doesn't this suggest the car would be remaining the same for the foreseeable future?

Above
Swish interior of TATA (Tenth Anniversary Trans Am) is silver-dyed leather. Seats were quite supportive, maybe not quite in top European sports car class, but pretty good. TATA possessed more luxury comfort and convenience items than found in a Rolls

Left
Three Tenth Anniversary Trans Ams were lent to Nascar to pace the 1979 Daytona 500 race held on 18 February. Although the standard TATA supposedly retailed for $10,620, some were selling for as high as $30,000!

A total of 22 years made up two generations of Firebirds. They went racing with so-so results, and they evolved into cars everybody could have fun with. There were bad sides, of course. One of the worst was lamentable quality that was sometimes so bad, road testers returned the cars. By 1990, workmanship had improved to the point that Firebirds were equal to the best of them.

It was to be hoped that the improved workmanship would remain for the new, fourth generation Firebird waiting in the wings.

Above
Black and white paint and special white wheels distinguish the 25th Anniversary car. Wheelbase is shorter by seven inches, to 101.1, and overall length is down 6.9 in. to 189.9 over the second generation models. Weight was also trimmed 435 lbs

Left
Trans Ams must have had more anniversary and special edition cars than anyone else. Here's the 1983 25th Anniversary Daytona 500 Pace Car. All new third Generation Firebird/Trans Am bowed in 1982. Front end of T/A is somewhat reminiscent of Star Wars' Darth Vada

Above left
First came the 10th Anniversary, then the 15th. To add lustre, there was the Pontiac Trans Am 100, paced naturally by a Trans Am, held as one of the races preceding the Detroit GP in 1984

Left
Interior of pace car replica was very business-like. Recaro style seats had excellent support, and were very comfortable. Optional engine for 1982/83 was the twin throttle-body fuel-injected 5-litre V-8, but the 4 bbl carbureted version was quicker

Above
Stylish rear end has lights concealed behind horizontal, colour keyed spokes. Model benefits greatly from much aerodynamic research in its overall design. Even rear spoiler is designed to smooth out turbulence leaving car

Above left

1985 Trans Am. Schinella and his design team wanted 'grunt' coupled with lean flowing lines. From its racy front with flush fitted headlight covers, the Trans Am stole the pony-car laurels

Left

Interior is functional yet comfortable. Door pulls are part of the arm rests and standard floor console has storage space above window lift buttons

Above

New taillights lose horizontal bars for cross-hatch design in the deep red plastic. Rear window louvers were a popular after-market option, helped with sun protection for rear passengers sitting under large expanse of glass

Right

5-litre High Output V-8 with tuned-port fuel injection developed 190 bhp in '85

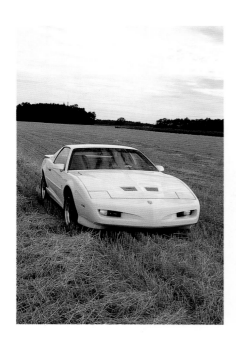

Above

With the exception of small modifications to front and rear, there had been few visible changes to Firebird/Trans Am models since 1982. A final facelift was given to the nine year old body for the 1991 model year

Right

There is something very embryonic about the way the front droops over the spoiler – was there a tadpole in somebody's subconscious? The 1991 GTA has 5.7 litre fuel injected V-8. Note how rear spoiler flares from base of window. 16 x 8 in. gold metallic wheels were standard on GTA

Above

Smart interior of 1992 Formula smacks more of luxury than sportiness. Seats are velour, but transmission is a 5-speed standard engine in the Formula was the fuel injected 5.0 litre developing 170 hp

Right

1992 Formula Hi-tech Turbo wheels, 5.0 litre power, 5-speed transmission. This was the final year for the third generation body style that had been around since 1982. 1992 was the Firebird's 25th anniversary which was celebrated with the first convertible since 1969

Above
Formula sports classic Trans Am 'power bulge' hood with lettering denoting engine size. Bulge was on left hand side of hood, and had scoop at the rear. Two other V-8 engines were offered; a 5.0 litre developing 225 hp and a 5.7L putting out 240 horses

Right
By 1992 carburetors had become redundant, their throne toppled by an industry swing to more efficient fuel injection. Just as in this 1992 Formula, engine bays had become increasingly crowded to the point where one could barely find one spark plug, let alone eight!

"Lethal ... 'n lovin' it"

Production of the 1993 fourth generation Firebird began in November 1992 at the GM Ste-Therese assembly plant in Quebec to enable enough stocks to be built up in readiness for the model's dealer showroom launch early in the new year. The automotive press had already seen and driven the eagerly awaited car, and what they experienced they generally liked.

Pontiac's press release on the new models – Firebird, Formula and Trans Am – claimed 90% of the car was all-new, including two new engines, a stronger, fortified base and dent, and rust resistant body panels made from lightweight polymer composite sheet molding compound. Only the hood and rear quarter panels were steel, and two sided galvanized steel at that! "Firebird has always symbolized the epitome of Pontiac sports car driving excitement," said Pontiac General Manager John G. Middlebrook. "Just like the two million units before it, the fourth generation will carry on that tradition ... cars designed to put fun and excitement in the driving experience."

Words couched in the ad man's vernacular are often cynical at best, quite untrue at worst. In the case of Mr Middlebrook's statement, however, the truth comes shining through the rhetoric. For more than a quarter of a century, Firebirds have satisfied and excited millions of buyers, teenage sons and daughters, and those who wished they could afford one. A look at the latest in the line has Pontiac's favourite word "excitement" written all over it. The shape is blatantly sexual, Freudian almost – its long, tapering, pointed front softly rounded in all the right places. "Its lethal ... but I love it," exclaimed one young woman after driving a 1994 model for the first time. "The car has an international design flavour to it," said Jack Folden, successor to John Schinella as Pontiac Exterior Studio II design chief, "and yet it very much says, 'I'm an American and proud of it'."

Designed and built in America (and Canada) nobody denies, yet there's just a touch of Italian and Japanese architecture in the final shape. Norm Fugate, director of validation? [author's question mark!] and development, admits to many miles with Toyota's 'world class' Supra

1993 fourth generation Firebird clothed in the mantle of night. New styling was evolutionary rather than revolutionary; wheelbase and length virtually unaltered. A Rustproof material, Sheet Molding Compound, was used on doors, roof and rear hatch

during the development of the latest Firebird. There is little doubt, and the designers happily agree, that much of the styling was heavily influenced by Pontiac's 1988 Banshee IV and ACC California Camaro concept cars.

Development of the fourth generation F-bodied Firebird and Camaro really began in 1988. Harvey Bell was chief engineer, Ted Robertson, platform engineering director, and Norm Fugate we already know. On the body and interior design there was Jack Folden (exterior), Bill Scott, chief designer, interior, Tom Peters, chief designer, Advanced #4 studio, with assistant, Dave Rand. These were the main body of men who brought the new Firebird to fruition. Overseeing the design operation was Chuck Jordan, vice-president of GM Design Staff, now retired.

Bearing in mind the original Banshee concept car was a forerunner to the first Firebird, and that each succeeding Banshee played its part in the development of each generation of Firebirds, it was natural that the latest one greatly influenced the design of the production car. "We were getting ready to design a whole new generation of image cars for Pontiac" said Folden, "and we wanted to test the waters. With Banshee, we made a statement about what the next generation of Firebird might look like. The overwhelming positive public reaction told us to go for it." Having been involved with Firebird design since 1974, Folden understands the strong emotional appeal the car has for the design staff. From the very beginning the Firebird has had this commitment from all those who worked to bring each generation to life. "We wanted to do a direction," recalls Folden, "because the Firebird, it's an interesting project whenever we get into it because it has such a strong visual and emotional tie with everybody that everyone wants to work on it. It's one of those projects that, you know, it doesn't come around that often and – boy – you want to be involved in it."

Once the go-ahead was given to design the fourth generation Firebird, Chuck Jordan told Folden and other designers to express what they felt, it wouldn't matter how wild the ideas were. "Be brave," Jordan said. Dozens of sketches and scale models later, all directions were pointing to the Banshee. As the team were working on the new car, the finishing touches were being done to the facelift of the 1991 model. Again the front was inspired by the Banshee. A full size mock-up was made of the proposed Firebird and Chuck Jordan was invited to view it. He could also see the facelifted third generation which helped him

Pontiac claims that the 1993 interior "shows the engineering commitment to a proper driving environment and intuitive operation". Star Trek door panels are handsome, as is heavily shrouded dashboard. Steering wheel shows optional radio controls on thick hub. Dual air bags were standard

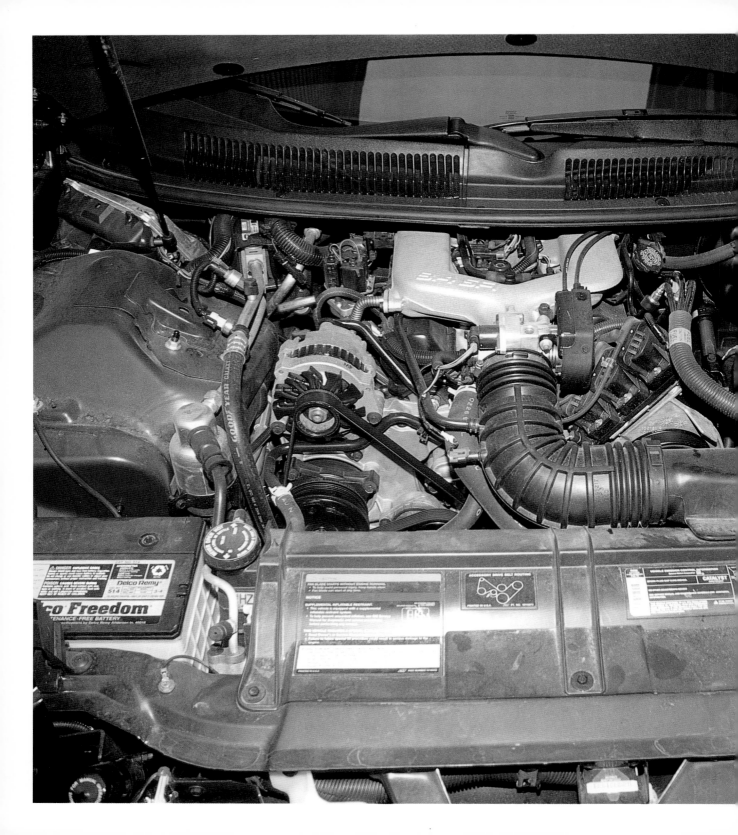

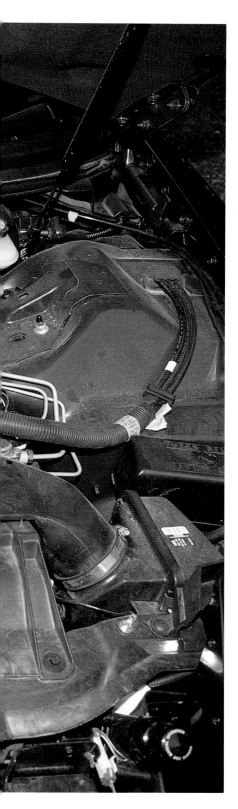

realize the Banshee show car influence was the way to go.

Working within the confines of a budget and having to share the F-body with Chevrolet can prove extremely difficult. As Folden says, a lot of the shapes couldn't have been accomplished had the cars been standard sheet metal. As it was, the new models used a great deal of composite plastic materials similar to the late and much lamented Fiero. The designers were able to bend and shape the plastic components enough to make Camaro and Firebird quite different from each other. With American auto manufacturers turning their attention increasingly towards both East and West Europe as a profitable export market, their cars are being designed with more of an international flavour. Pontiac expects to sell at least three or four thousand Firebirds annually to Europe and elsewhere. Unfortunately EEC (European Economic Community) countries don't see eye-to-eye with the Americans when it

Above
A warm summer's evening in the famous town of Marshall, Michigan. The fountain shimmers under a cloak of water playing on its pillars

Left
Gone are the days when engine maintenance was an uncomplicated procedure. Open the hood of any modern car and one is faced by a nightmare whereby one almost needs a degree to work out where the plugs are. This is the Firebird 3.4 litre V6, believe it or not!

comes to safety. This has to be added, that has to be taken off. Very silly, but American designers have to comply with these regulations if the car is to be sold in Europe. Any protrusions or body angularity deemed by the Europeans to be harmful to humans in an impact have to be rounded off, and outside rear mirrors have to break away cleanly from the body.

Trying to understand the minds of the people who work for governmental bureaucracies is as easy as trying to read Webster's Dictionary in Chinese … after one five minute lesson. People have been driven to drink trying to fathom them out. Surely the safety measures laid down by the U.S. authorities have undergone numerous tests before being made law. Why these aggravating little differences? Either a Europeans' molecular structure is different from Americans or, and much more likely, it's petty revenge against the U.S. authorities' insistence that EEC cars must comply with American regulations.

Satisfying GM's Overseas Distribution Corp. is one thing; satisfying others such as the engineers, is another. One item that almost didn't make it was the steeply raked windshield, which is angled at 68°. Folden and his team knew the design of the Firebird called for a radically sloping windshield. Without it, the car wouldn't look right.

Engineering didn't see it that way. They said getting the air to flow through the cowl vent would be tricky, and the windshield wipers would lift at speed. Jack Folden again: "We were a big advocate of trying to get this very smooth profile … we didn't know all of the engineering effort that it would require of the platform and ourselves. "We spent more hours in the wind tunnel and on the test track trying to make sure that we got the wipers so that they would work and I think they wanted something like at 140 mph the wipers still had to stick tight to the windshield." Eventually a wiper arm strong enough to hold the wipers down at speeds of up to 100 mph was designed, the cowl problem solved and the design team got the windshield.

Bill Scott was Pontiac chief interior designer at the time the fourth generation Firebird was taking shape. His job was to create an interior to match the exterior. He and his interior team worked in conjunction with

Right
Guess what Pontiac did for the Trans Am's 25th birthday? Built a 25th Anniversary edition, of course! Production was kept to 2000 units to make the car truly special. White Prado leather seats with blue embroidery were exclusive to this car

Overleaf
You might be able to make out '25 Trans Am' on the side of this special anniversary car as it hurtles out of the picture. Standard V8 for Formula and Trans Am models is a 275 bhp OHV, 5.7 litre unit capable of reaching 150 mph

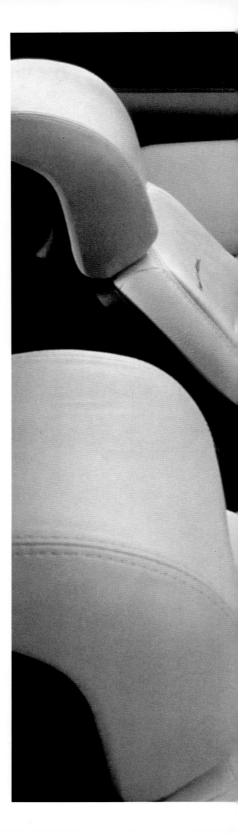

the exterior design staff in the exterior design studio. By taking this unusual and radical step – interior and exterior normally work independently of each other – both sides understood what the other was looking for, thus resulting in a car that blended every which way to create a cohesive whole. Following the smooth flow of the exterior, Bill Scott and his boys matched it with a rounded, curvaceous interior that would appeal both to the performance minded and discriminating followers of fashion. A large, legible instrument cluster with analog gauges, are positioned directly in front of the driver's eyes. The sound system and all major controls can be reached without the driver having to lean forward in his seat.

Seats are ergonomically contoured with a range of adjustments to suit even the pickiest of drivers, and the six-speed manual transmission or four-speed automatic shifter set in the center console, fall naturally to hand. Like everyone else now seems to, the Firebird has what is called environmentally friendly air conditioning. The new chlorine-free refrigerant replaces freon, long known to be hazardous to the environment. It's a blessing to see the back of freon, and it is about time too. And while we're discussing safety, both driver and front passenger have air bags as standard. Energy-absorbing instrument panel and front seatback tops, and three point safety belts are a couple more of the many new safety features to be found in the latest Firebird.

There are three models – Firebird, Formula and Trans Am. The Firebird is the base car and is powered by a 160 hp 3.4 litre V-6; this engine replaces the previous 3.1 litre V-6 and has the advantage of 20 more horsepower. The only engine available for both Formula and Trans Am is the LT1 275 hp 5.7 litre ohv V-8 courtesy Chevrolet Corvette. Mated to the Borg-Warner six-speed manual this engine more than makes up for the days when a Trans Am had a massive 455 under the hood.

Of the three models, the Trans Am is the most spectacular in terms of standard equipment. There are just five options: automatic transmission, leather seats, compact disc player, removable hatch roof and sunshades. Pontiac is targeting the Trans Am at those with salaries of $45,000 or more. Gone – long gone – is the great big, flattened 'screaming chicken' decal from the hood. Pontiac believes the car is too sophisticated for '60s-type symbolism. As for the Formula, it is not quite the same as the Trans Am, even though it shares the same engine and suspension. Both the Firebird and Formula are approximately one inch shorter and have larger, flared 'nostrils' than the Trans Am which has two deep, round recesses housing the parking lights.

When the fourth generation Firebird was first decided upon, GM was considering turning it into a front-wheel-drive car. Resistance to this proposal soon had placed the idea in a kind of limbo. Surveys had shown that Firebird enthusiasts overwhelmingly preferred the traditional front engine, rear drive format – old fashioned or not. A lot of changes took place under the skin. First Pontiac engineers tossed out the MacPherson independent front suspension in favour of an unequal-length control-arm system popularly known as the short/long arm (SLA) type. Due to its design, the suspension delivers lateral control with infinitely improved ride quality.

At the rear is the old Salisbury solid axle with a torque arm extending from the differential housing, through the transmission tunnel, its front end bolting to the transmission housing. Coil springs are located behind the axle tubes, the gas pressurized shocks ahead of it. The axle is positioned by two trailing arms and a transverse track bar. A 19mm anti-roll bar completes the picture for the Formula and Trans Am. The same set up can be found on the Firebird except the anti-roll bar is 17mm. Both Formula and Trans Am have four-wheel disc brakes as standard, while the base Firebird has disc/drums. All models sport ABS as standard. Power rack and pinion steering replaces the time-honoured recirculating ball system which is more suited to large, antedeluvian Fleetwoods than to sportier cars. Surprisingly, Mercedes-Benz still swears by recirculating ball.

A new President, a new direction and a recession finally starts to recede. Car sales improve dramatically in 1993; the all-new Firebird and Camaro doing very well. A much more confident motor industry heads into 1994 with sales still up. Sharing that confidence is the Firebird with two exceptional new models guaranteed to turn excitement levels even higher. One is the return of the convertible, the other a very special 25th Anniversary Trans Am.

All models from the base Firebird to the Trans Am are available as convertibles, including a handful of 25th Anniversary editions. The convertibles have a power top that folds flush and is stored beneath a three-piece tonneau cover. With the top up, there's a glass rear window with electric defogger, and a fully trimmed headliner helps to cut down the noise associated with convertible tops when they're up. "Pontiac will only build around 2,000 of the 25th Anniversary Trans Ams," said Pontiac General Manager John G. Middlebrook. Which of course meant that every one of these cars which paced the 1994 Daytona 500 would be instantly snapped up. Hardly surprising really. The model was available in white only, with a bright blue centreline strip, white aluminum 16 in.

A beautiful car. The 1994 Formula, however, not only has beauty but state-of-the-art sophistication as well. This, and the power the car has on tap, appeal to those who wish, as Pontiac puts it, to be "driving excitement"

wheels, white leather seats with blue embroidery, and had virtually every extra that Pontiac could toss at it. Only three options were available in this car: four-speed automatic, compact disc player, and T-tops with sunshades.

There's little doubt that the fourth generation Firebird is the best of the bunch. A drive in one will soon convince even the hardest of souls that here is a unique and beautiful car. Wherever it is driven it attracts attention, possibly because the heady rumbling of the V-8 invites heads to turn. One area Pontiac seem to have cured is the poor quality that Firebirds were endowed with. Cars built in the seventies were especially bad, though one could make the excuse there really was not much incentive to put cars together particularly well during that sad decade. The latest models are beautifully put together, with well fitted doors, hoods and trim, and an equally good finish on the interior.

Take a long dry stretch, rev the 5.7 litre engine, slip the clutch, drop into first, and … vroom! … shades of the muscle bound sixties come flooding back. Red-line at 6000 rpm, into second, the engine's response is immediate. Into third, fourth, fifth, and sixth. The faster one shifts, the smoother the shifts. There's none of that woolly feel associated with some manual transmissions. Borg-Warner has developed a beautiful box that shifts with precision, each shift very positive, even for critical European tastes.

A 160 mph speedometer surely invites trouble on America's 65 mph interstates – the state police watch for low slung, lithe shapes like the new Firebird to come into view, routinely blipping them with their radar guns. 0–60 in the 1994 Formula is a rapid 6.3 seconds and the car is still galloping at 140 mph. This car is fun, fun, fun. There are disadvantages that have been lived with and can still be lived with. No matter what the engineers try to do, a torquey, heavyweight cast-iron V-8 will always give a rigid rear axle the jitters. Although Pontiac has made great strides with the Firebird, the fact remains that the stiff suspension will set up an uncomfortable judder on poorly surfaced roads. And the tail will whip from side to side like an angry alligator when power is suddenly applied. Even with Goodyear Eagle P245/502R-16 tires the tremendous torque still has to be reined in. As the lady said: "Lethal …"

We haven't mentioned Firebird's competitive spirit too much because this book is about road-going 'birds. However a quick survey of the marque's racing activities won't go amiss. After all, the Trans Am was named after the Sports Car Club of America's Trans American

Yes, that's a 275 bhp V-8 in there – but how does anybody manage to work on it if the occasion arises? Engine is buffered by crumple-zone technology which saves lives in the event of an accident

Championship, and as we saw in the first chapter, Canadian millionaire Terry Godsall and driving partner, Jerry Titus, were the first to race the marque with moderate success.

Stock car racing luminary, Buck Baker, drove a Firebird to victory in NASCAR's Grand American series, in 1969. The following year Baker posted two more wins, and in 1971 snatched three more victories. In 1972, Trans Ams driven by Tiny Lund and Dave Paschal scored wins, while Dave Pearson and Lund grabbed a few second place finishes. Buck Baker scored one third place. Still, it was enough to enable a proud Trans Am to walk off with the coveted manufacturer's championship.

Pontiac engineer, Herb Adams, loved motorsports. He had enough faith in Trans Ams to race them. He and some friends put $1,000 each into a kitty and formed Team Associates. They then built a racing car out of a crashed Trans Am. One first, several second and third places, assured Pontiac of finishing third in the manufacturer's championship. Herb Adams left Pontiac in 1973, and set himself up in racing. He built a special car called the Silverbird. Very loosely based on the Firebird, the Silverbird didn't do particularly well, partly because funds were tight. At an event in Laguna Seca, California, Adams' Silverbird, driven by Milt Minter, humiliated a strong Porsche challenge, and came in second behind a Corvette.

In the late sixties and early seventies, Trans Ams went on the funny car circuit to compete in drag racing. Jess Tyree was a drag racing institution and, between 1967 and 1975, brought home the bacon with a 75% win rate. In the eighties, from 1982 to '89, another big drag racer, Don 'The Snake' Prudhomme won 10 NHRA National events with a Trans Am funny car. Another dragster who made a success out of driving Trans Am funny cars, was 'Bad' Brad Anderson. He scored 16 NHRA National event wins.

Although Firebirds and Trans Ams have competed very successfully in NHRA Super Stock and drag racing, perhaps the most prestigious events are the record breaking trysts on the Bonneville Salt Flats. In 1986, a GTA built by Gale Banks, an aftermarket turbocharger specialist, and partner Bruce Geisler, became the world's fastest passenger car on August 20th when it posted a two way average of 260.210 mph. The car, driven by Salt Flats veteran, Don Stringfellow, returned the following year to try and crack the elusive 300 mph barrier. Stringfellow pushed the record to 268.033.

Pontiac generously supports these attempts on cracking the 300 mph

Rear of Formula is a beautiful piece of design, with rounded shapes flowing into one another. Even the spoiler is integrated into the overall shape. Car has Pass-Key II Theft Deterrent System which has helped reduce thefts considerably

barrier with a Firebird. To be the holder of the 300 mph record would be a tremendous feather in anybody's cap. Naturally Pontiac wants it to be *its* cap. In 1989 Pontiac supported another effort to crack the record. John Lingenfelter, the well known racing engine builder, teamed up with Karl Staggemeier and Gary Eaker and went to the flats with a 1989 Trans Am. They broke the existing record with a two way average of 293.150 mph. Other attempts failed to better that run, although there are many still making the attempt to be the first to crack the elusive 300!

What of the future for Pontiac's only rear drive car? At this point with everything coming up roses for the latest Firebird, who knows. It hardly seems likely that there will be many changes for the next six or seven years – this writer believes the next all-new Firebird will be in the year 2000. Pontiac's enthusiastic, and very talented team know they can't go much further with the present layout, so maybe we will see IRS at last. As Jaguar, Mercedes, and Rolls-Royce have successfully proved, one doesn't need front-wheel-drive to have IRS.

Whatever. Considering one can buy a new Formula for as little as $17,995, the six-cylinder version for $13,995, the Firebird is the best bargain sports car money can buy. Even with its few imperfections there really is nothing to touch it. You see, the magic of the Firebird is its personality, that intangible something special that the oh-so-perfect Japanese sports cars strive for but can't match.

Firebirds equate fun, fun, fun. And that is what a sports car is about.

1994 Formula can really move when it is allowed ... which is not often bearing in mind state troopers' eagle eyes and radar guns that are ever-present on the interstates. European buyers have the advantage of the Autobahn to savour Formula's speed. For true value, no other sportscar could match the Formula's bargain $17,995 price

Specifications

1967

Models: Sprint, 326, 326 H.O., 400, 400.
Engines: Sohc I-6, 230 cid., compression ratio, 9.0:1, 165 hp. sohc, I-6, 230 cid., cr. 10.5:1, 215 hp. V-8, 326 cid., cr. 9.2:1, 250 hp. V-8, 326 cid., cr. 10.75:1, 285 hp. V-8, 400 cid, cr. 10.75:1, 325 hp, V-8, 400 cid, cr. 10.75:1, 325 hp*
*(1400 developed max, hp. at 4800 rpm, the other at 5200 rpm).
Wheelbase: 108.1, length 188.8.
Price: $2,666 to $2,903. (prices vary with inclusion of options)

1968

Models: Sprint, 350, 350 H.O., 400, 400.
Engines: Sohc I-6, 250 cid., cr. 9.0:1, 175 bhp. sohc I-6, 250 cid, 215 bhp, cr. 10.5:1. V-8, 350 cid, 265 bhp, cr. 9.2:1. V-8, 350 cid, 320 bhp, cr. 10.5:1. V-8, 400 cid, 330 bhp. cr. 10.8:1. V-8, 400 cid, 335 bhp, cr. 10.8:1. (A high performance 400 developed 340 bhp).
Wheelbase: 108.1, length 188.8.
Price: $2,781 to $2,996.

1969

Models: Sprint, 350, 350 H.O., 400, 400. (Trans Am was options package at this point).
Engines: sohc I-6, 250 cid, 215 bhp, cr. 9.0:1. sohc I-6, 250 cid, 215 bhp, cr 10.5:1. V-8, 350 cid, 265 bhp, cr. 9.2:1. V-8, 350 cid, 325 bhp, cr. 10.5:1. V-8 400 cid, 330 bhp, cr. 10.75:1. V-8, 400 cid, 335 bhp, cr. 10.75:1. (High performance version developed 345 bhp).
Wheelbase: 101.1, length 188.8.
Price: $2,821 to $3,045.

1970

Models: Firebird, Esprit, Esprit, Formula, Trans Am.
Engines: ohv I-6, 250 cid, 155 bhp, cr. 8.5:1. V-8, 350 cid, 255 bhp, cr. 8.8:1. V-8, 400 cid, 265 bhp, cr. 8.8:1. V-8, 400 cid, 330 bhp, cr. 10.25:1. V-8, 400 cid, 335 bhp, cr. 10.5:1. V-8, 400 cid, 345 bhp, cr. 10.75:1.
Wheelbase: 108 in., length, 191.6 in.
Price: $2,875 to $4,305.

1971

Models: Firebird, Esprit, Formula, Trans Am.
Engines: ohv I-6, 250 cid, 145 bhp, cr. 8.5:1. V-8, 350 cid, 250 bhp, cr. 8.0:1. V-8, 400 cid, 265 bhp, cr. 8.2:1. V-8, 400 cid, 300 bhp, cr. 8.2:1. V-8, 455 cid, 325 bhp, cr 8.2:1. V-8, 455 cid, 335 bhp, 8.4:1.
Wheelbase: 108 in., length, 191.6 in.
Price: $3,047 to $4,595.

1972

Models: Firebird, Esprit, Formula, Trans Am.
Note. From 1972 the American motor industry changed over to SAE net horsepower ratings. Before 1972 American cars' horsepower ratings were given in gross output figures. Net is for a complete engine
Engines: I-6, 250 cid, 110 bhp, cr. 8.5:1. V-8, 350 cid, 160 & 175 bhp, cr. 8.0:1 (both). V-8, 400 cid, 175 & 250 bhp, cr. 8.2:1 (both). V-8, 455 cid, 300 bhp, cr. 8.4:1.
Wheelbase: 108 in., length, 191.6 in.
Price: $2,828 to $4,256.

1973

Models: Firebird, Esprit, Formula, Trans Am.
Engines: I-6, 250 cid, 110 bhp, cr. 8.2:1. V-8 350 cid, 150 & 175 bhp, cr. 7.6:1 (both). V-8, 400 cid, 170 & 230 hp, cr. 8.0:1 (both). V-8, 455 cid, 250 bhp, cr. 8.0:1. V-8, 455 cid Super Duty, 310 bhp, cr. 8.4:1.
Wheelbase: 108 in., length, 192.1.
Price: $2,895 to $4,204

1974

Models: Firebird, Esprit, Formula, Trans Am.
Engines: I-6, 250 cid, 110 bhp, cr. 8.2:1. V-8, 350 cid, 155 & 170 bhp cr. 7.6:1 (both). V-8, 400 cid, 175, 190, & 225 bhp, cr. 8.0:1 (all).V-8 455 cid, 250 bhp, cr. 8.0:1. V-8, 455 cid, 290 bhp, cr. 8.4:1.
Wheelbase: 108 in., length, 196.in.
Price: $3,335 to $4,446.

1975

Models: Firebird, Esprit, Formulas, Trans Am.
Engines: I-6, 250 cid, 105 bhp, cr. 8.3:1. V-8, 350 cid, 155 & 175 bhp, cr. 7.6:1 (both). V-8, 400 cid, 185 bhp, cr. 7.6:1. V-8, 455 cid, 200 bhp, cr. 7.6:1.
Wheelbase: 108 in, length 196 in.
Price: $3,713 to $4,740.

1976

Models: As before.
Engines: I-6, 250 cid, 110 bhp, cr. 8.3:1. V-8, 350 cid, 160 & 165 bhp, cr. 7.6:1 (both). V-8, 400 cid, 185 bhp, cr. 7.6:1. V-8, 455 cid, 200 bhp, cr. 7.6:1.
Wheelbase: 108.1 in., length, 196.8 in.
Price: $3,906 to $4,987.

1977

Models: As before.
Engines: V-6, 231 cid, 105 bhp, cr. 8.0:1. V-8, 301 cid, 135 bhp, cr. 8.2:1. V-8, 350 cid, 170 bhp, cr. 7.6:1. V-8, 400 cid, 180 bhp, cr. 7.6:1. V-8, 400 cid, 200 bhp, cr. 8.0:1. V-8, 403 cid, 185 bhp, cr. 8.0:1.
Wheelbase: As before.
Price: $4,270 to $5,456.

1978

Models: As before.
Engines: V-6, 231 cid, 105 bhp, cr. 8.0:1. V-8, 305 cid, 135 & 145 bhp, cr. 8.4:1 (both). V-8, 350 cid, 160 & 170 bhp, cr. 8.2:1 (both). V-8, 400 cid, 180 bhp, cr. 7.7:1. V-8, 400 cid, 220 bhp, cr. 8.1:1. V-8, 403 cid, 185 bhp, cr. 7.9:1.
Wheelbase: 108.2 in., length, 196.8 in.
Price: $4,593 to $5,889.

1979

Models: As before plus Trans Am Limited Edition.
Engines: 231 cid, 115 bhp, cr. 8.0:1. V-8, 301 cid, 135 bhp, cr. 8.1:1. V-8, 301 cid, 150 bhp, cr. 8.1. V-8, 305 cid, 125 bhp, cr. 8.4:1 V-8, 350 cid, 165 bhp, cr. 8.2:1. V-8 400 cid, 220 bhp, cr. 8.1:1. V-8, 455 cid, 185 bhp, cr. 7.9:1.
Wheelbase: 108.2 in., length 198.1 in.
Price: $5,260 to $10,620*
*The latter figure applied to T/A Special Edition only.

1980

Models: As before, minus Special Edition model.
Engines: V-6, 231 cid, 115 bhp, cr. 8.0:1. V-8, 265 cid, 120 bhp, cr. 8.3:1. V-8, 301 cid, 140 & 155 bhp, cr. 8.1:1. V-8 Turbo, 301 cid, 210 bhp, cr. 7.6:1. V-8, 305 cid, 150 bhp, cr. 8.4:1.
Wheelbase: As before.
Price: $5,948 to $7,480.

1981

Models: As before plus special edition T/A turbo coupe.
Engines: V-6, 231 cid ... as before. V-8, 265 cid ... as before.V-8, 301 cid, 150 bhp, cr. 8.1:1. Turbo V-8, 301 cid, 200 bhp, cr. 7.5:1. V-8, 305 cid, 145 bhp, cr. 8.6:1.
Wheelbase: As before.
Price: $6,901 to $8,322 (Trans Am Turbo Coupe SE cost $12,257).

Please note: The American auto industry joined the rest of the world by describing engine sizes in litres instead of cubic inches.

1982

Models: Firebird, Firebird Trans Am, Firebird S/E.
Engines: I-4, 2.5L., 90 bhp, cr. 8.2:1. V-6, 2.8L., 105 bhp, cr. 8.5:1. V-8, 5.0L., 150 bhp, cr. 8.6:1. V-8 with throttle-body fuel injection, 5.0L., 165 bhp, cr. 8.6:1.
Wheelbase: 101 in., length, 189.8 in.
Price: $7,996 to $9.658.

1983

Models: Firebird, Trans Am, Firebird S/E.
Engines: I-4, 2.5L., 90 bhp, cr. 8.2:1. V-6, 2.8L., 105 bhp, (an H.O. version was available with 135 bhp), cr. 8.5:1. V-8, 5.0L., 150 bhp, cr. 8.6:1. V8, H.O., 190 bhp, cr. 8.6:1.
Wheelbase: As before.
Price: $8.399 to $10,397.

1984

Models: Firebird, Trans Am, Firebird S/E.
Engines: I.4, 2.5L., 92 bhp, cr. 9.0:1. V-6, 2.8L, 107 bhp, cr. 8.5:1. V-6, 2.8L, 125 bhp, cr. 8.9:1. V-8, 5.0L, 145 bhp, cr. 8.6:1. V-8, 5.0L 190 bhp, cr. 9.5:1.
Wheelbase: 101 in, length, 189.8 in.

1985

Models: As before.
Engines: I-4, 2.5L., 88 bhp, cr. 9.0:1. V-6, 2.8L., 135 bhp., cr. 8.9:1. V-8, 5.0L., 150, cr. 8.6:1. V-8, 5.0L., 190 bhp, cr. 9.5:1. V-8, 5.0L., 210 bhp, cr. 9.0:1.
Wheelbase: As above with the exception of the Trans Am which had an overall length of 191.6 in.
Price: $8,679 to $11,335.

1986

Models: As before.
Engines: As 1985.
Wheelbase: As before
Prices: $9,279 to $12,395.

1987

Models: Firebird (Coupe, Formula Coupe), Trans Am (Coupe, GTA Coupe).
Engines: V-6, 2.8L., 135 bhp, cr. 8.9:1. V-8, 5.0L, 155, 165, and 205 bhp, cr. 9.3:1 (all). V-8, 5.7L., 210 bhp, cr. 9.3:1.
Wheelbase: 101 in., length, 188 in (191.6 in. on Trans Am).
Price: $10,359 to $13,259.

1988

Models: As before.
Engines: V-6, 2.8L., 135 bhp, cr. 8.5:1. V.8, 5.0L, 190, 215 bhp, cr. 9.3:1. V-8, 5.7L., 225 bhp, cr. 9.3:1.
Wheelbase: As before.
Price: $10,999 to $19,299.

1989

Models: As before plus limited edition 20th Anniversary T/A.
Engines: V-6, 2.8L., 135 bhp, cr. 8.5:1. V-6, 3.8L. turbo-charged, 250 bhp, cr. 8.0:1. V-8 5.0L., 215 and 225 bhp, cr. 9.3:1 (both). V-8, 5.7L., 225 and 235 bhp, cr. 9.3:1 (both).
Wheelbase: As before.
Price: $11,999 to $20,339.

1990

Models: As before minus 20th Ann. T/A.
Engines: V-6, 3.1L., 140 bhp, cr. 8.5:1. V-8, 5.0L., 170, 205, & 225 bhp, cr. 9.3:1 (all). V-8, 5.7L. 235 bhp, cr. 9.3:1.
Wheelbase: As before.
Price: $11,320 to $23,320.

1991

Models: As before.
Engines: As before.
Wheelbase: 101 in., length 195.1 in.
Price: $12,690 to $24,530.

1992

Models: As before.
Engines: As before
Wheelbase: As before

1993

Models: Firebird, Formula, Trans Am.
Engines: V-6, 3.4L., 160 bhp, cr. 9.1:0. V-8, 5.7L., 275 bhp. cr. 10.3:1.
Wheelbase: 101.1 in., length, 195.6 (197.0 in. for Trans Am).

1994

Models: As before with addition of limited edition 25th Anniversary Trans Am.
Engines: See 1993.
Wheelbase: See 1993

Production Figures

Year	Base		Esprit	Formula	Trans Am		Total
1967	2H	67032					
	2C	15528					
	T	82560					82560
1968	2H	90152					
	2C	16960					
	T	107112					107112
1969	2H	75370			2H	689	
	2C	11649			2C	8	
	T	87019			T	697	87716
1970	37835			7708	3196		48739
1971	23021		20185	7802	2116		53124
1972	12000		11415	5250	1286		29951
1973	14096		17249	10166	4802		46313
1974	26372		22583	14519	10255		73729
1975	22293		20826	13670	27274		84063
1976	21209		22252	20613	46701		110775
1977	30642		34548	21801	68745		155736
1978	32672		36926	24346	93341		187285
1979	38642		30853	24850	117109		211454
1980	29811		17277	9356	50896		107340
1981	20542		10939	5926	33492		70899
1982	41683			21719	52960		116362
1983	32020			10934	31930		74884
1984	62621			10309	55374		128304
1985	46644			5208	44028		95880
1986	59334			2259	48870		110463
1987	42558		13164	11102	21788		88612
1988	28973		13475	11214	8793		62455
1989	32376		16670	9631	5727*		64404
1990	13212		4834	1447	1060		20553
1991	37762		5544	2915	4013		50234
1992	24364		1052	508	1643		27567

1993 overall production was 16,175. **Projected 1994** figures are 55,000.

*1555 Special edition 20th anniversary Indy pace cars included in the figure

Source, Pontiac Motor Division.

Recommended reading

The Fabulous Firebird, Michael Lamm (Lamm-Morada Publishing Co)

Pontiac. They Build Excitement, Thomas Bonsall (Stony Run Press)

Road & Track, Motor Trend, Car Life, Automobile, Collectible Automobile

Consumer Guide Auto Test Annuals, 1973 to 1994 (Publications International)